Will the Real Me, Please Stand Up!

By

Narda Goodson

5/19/2012
Carole Mitchell -
May the words in
this book bring you
encouragement + may it
breathe life into your
dreams! :)

Narda Goodson
First Lady of
Whitewright, Texas

NG

Dedication

Mi Amor, the one I love, my husband Bill – Our life has been a love story from the moment we met. You are my 21st century Boaz and my kinsman redeemer. I know that I have been creatively designed and anointed to be your woman because my past was preparing and teaching me how to love you. As our yesterdays have prepared us for our today and tomorrows, together let us make our mark on God's historical timeline.

You are an amazing person to know and I am honored to be your wife. The humility that flows from your heart causes you to stand tall and in my eyes, you will always be my hero and my champion. Thank you for all the love and support you showed me during the writing of this book. I could not have done it without you. Truly, the Lord has given me beauty for ashes, strength for fear, gladness for mourning and peace for despair.

To my daughters, my Anointed Arrows - Sade, Shanette and Shayna – being your mother has been the greatest calling in my life. It has been rewarding to watch you develop over the years and blossom into the beautiful young ladies you are today.

You have been my inspiration during the times I wanted to give up and concede defeat. But I have battled and defeated the many giants in the land so that you can now enter into the promises of the kingdom and enjoy the spoils. Now you will face the new horizons but conquer the impossibilities and allow the challenges of life to make you and not break you; for our trials only come to make us strong. When you are tested, take courage, when you are faced with opposition, fight tenaciously and when you are persecuted and ostracized remember God has already given you the victory.

I prophesy and declare you to be women of virtue and of excellence. You shall stand before the great and the noble to declare the Word of the Lord. You shall increase in wisdom and blossom in prosperity. Your voices shall be as the sounds of many trumpets and your gifts will make room for you.

I call you **Anointed Arrows**, God's massive tool that will wreak havoc on the kingdom of darkness. As I pass the baton, fight the good fight of faith and let no man take your crown. Fix your eyes on the prize and run this race with patience; for this race is not for the strong and mighty but only for those who endure to the end.

May your loins be swathed in truth, your heart engrossed with honesty and sincerity. Wisdom shall be your crown of glory and your lips oiled in pureness. Let your neck be laced with sound wisdom and discretion and your posture fortified in confidence. Stand for righteousness, love genuinely, pray fervently, serve with humility and give with simplicity. Stand for something so that you do not fall for anything.

DREAM my daughters, BELIEVE the impossible, and LIVE in expectancy…for with God ALL THINGS are POSSIBLE!

Acknowledgement

My mother, brothers and sisters – For too long did I allow the pain of my past to keep me from loving who God created me to be. I am sorry for never realizing how much it hurt you when I stayed away and didn't call. Because I have been restored to wholeness, I have come to love and celebrate my uniqueness. The '**real me**' isn't so bad after all. You are a big part of the 'real me' and I have discovered that I do have wonderful brothers and sisters who are funny and full of life and an extraordinary gem for a mother.

A special thanks to my mentors: Dr./Pastor Lucielle Green of *The Rock Ministries*, Teaneck, NJ, Pastors James & Michelle Lewis of *A Ray of Hope Ministries*, Snellville, GA, Pastors Reford & Sheri Mott of *Family Christian Center*, New Rochelle, NY, Pastor Keith Elijah & Yvonne Thompson of *Bronx Miracle Gospel Tabernacle*, Bronx, NY, Roslyn Lloyd Kennedy, Tampa, FL, and Pastor Ann Grant *Morrison*, Brooklyn, NY.

The role you played in my life was strategic and by the divine plan of God. From my Mordecai to the Naomi(s), and the mid-wives that help nurture and birth the ministry God placed in me; to my teachers and professors of hard-core discipleship and training… thank you for giving to the Lord. I have been called into the kingdom for such a time as this.

To His Glory Publishing Company – You are not just my publisher but my friends. Thank you for the hard work, support and prayers during the writing of this book.

Professor Soyini Richards Galimore – You have been a faithful comrade and dear friend. We have shared so many hardships, laughter and tears. Remember the hot days on the old Georgia road? How about the bread and coffee place? Those were some dark and gloomy days, but as we journeyed through our wilderness experience together, we were like two little girls looking through the eyes of faith; laughing, confessing and speaking to the "nothings" in our lives. Thank you for always seeing the best in me and never letting me forget that God had a bright future and an expected end for me. Well, it's so bright now, girl, I think we need our sunglasses.

Creflo Dollar Ministries – When my world around me began to fall apart, the anointing and the power of the online messages gave me repeated comfort, strength and support that empowered me to continue to believe in my dreams. Thank you…

Joyce Meyers Ministries – Joyce, you have been an incredible inspiration to me. I want to say thank you for keeping it real. What came to obliterate me of my destiny only propelled me into it.

Elder Clyde Stephens – I thank God for the day I met you on TBN's parking lot. Thank you for being obedient to the Lord. You were definitely a God-link.

My sisters and brothers in the Lord – Ruthven & Jackie Mereigh, Stacey-Ann Wakefield, Vivian Lavergne, Sheila Innis, Gina Barcourt, Tarsha Swindell, Pastor Raymond John, and Sean Phekoo. Your friendship, genuine prayers and love over the years will always be treasured in my heart. Thank you for believing in me during the roughest and toughest times of my Christian journey.

Endorsement

In this book, my wife Narda tells the reader about her personal experiences and how she struggled for years with an identity crisis and how she finally came full circle and embraced who she is, embraced her Spanish heritage and then stepped into the call of God on her life.

This is a must read for anyone who is facing many of life's challenges and a formula for overcoming rejection and betrayal. Many people will be healed by it and many lives will be changed by it.

—Mayor Bill Goodson
Whitewright, Texas

Will the Real Me, Please Stand Up!

All scriptures are quoted from the
King James Version of the Bible.

Published by: **To His Glory Publishing Company, Inc.**
463 Dogwood Drive, NW • Lilburn, GA 30047
(770) 458-7947 • www.tohisglorypublishing.com

Book is available at:
Amazon.com, BarnesandNoble.com,
Borders.com, Booksamillion.com etc.
You can also order this book through any of
your local bookstores.
For further information, contact:
www.tohisglorypublishing.com
(770) 458-7947

This book is also available in the
United Kingdom and Canada.

To contact the author/publisher, call (770) 458-7947

Cover Design By: To His Glory Publishing Co., Inc.

International Standard Book Number: 9780979156656

Table of Contents

Preface

The sound of Latin rhythms make me cry. Sorrow, grief, and hatred wraps itself around my heart like a warm blanket each time I hear what people say is the most beautiful music in the world. I hate it; it makes me sick to my stomach. I hate the culture, the food, the language and all that Latinos represent.

I do not comprehend the overwhelming anguish I sense each time I travel through the streets, hear the music, smell the food or see the people. I feel so repulsed toward my people, my culture because they only bring me distress and unhappy memories. How do I embrace the culture I was birthed into? How do I welcome into my life what I have resented and suppressed for years? My destiny is hidden in my history; for I am Puerto Rican, I am a Spanish woman and that is who I am created to be.

As I write this book, I am in the process of finding myself. The work has already begun. God has written the script for my life and now I must play the character; for He said the only way out is to go through. I am afraid of who I am because I have hidden her for so long. I do not know if I will recognize her or even like her when I meet her once again.

Chapter 1

I Declare War!

What do you do when unsuspecting trouble viciously knocks on the doors of your home? What do you do when the inconceivable takes place and what you never anticipated gruesomely and hauntingly stares you in the face? It tells you that war has been declared. Now what?

I know that this war is staged by the real enemy of my soul—satan. Therefore, if I am to outlive this adversity, I must tighten my armor, man my station and prepare for battle. For the enemy has threatened to obliterate my destiny. They (satan and his agents) have doggedly positioned themselves against me, defying the Captain of the Lord of Hosts.

The Vision of My Path:

The inescapable path is set before me as I am now compelled to smite the Goliaths dwelling in my land. While my enemies appear to be many, God has promised to strengthen and help me destroy them one by one. For He said He will uphold me with the saving strength of his right hand. He will contend with those that contend against me, and they shall be as nothing before me (Isaiah 41:10-11).

The battle cry has sounded and the alarm has been heard. I am summoned to war. As I stand on the front line of the battlefield and look ahead, my foes grimly gibe in hopes of bringing apprehension and a loss of composure toward my confidence in God. But I mark my position and steadfastly look on knowing that I am clothed in the Armor of God.

As a soldier, I knew that if I was going to outlive this adversity, I had to be covered with the various pieces of weaponry that God had designed to protect and equip me for fighting. I needed supernatural ability and strength that could only come from a higher source.

As I secured each piece of armor, my heart panted with anticipation; for my God had promised that the victory was already won through the blood that was shed on Calvary's Cross. When I began to exalt and eulogize the Lordship of my *Jehovah-Nissi,* in the Spirit, I heard the booming timbres of victory. An incomparable sanguine atmosphere was released as I praised and worshipped my Victor and Champion, Jesus Christ. As I lifted up my *Banner*, the streamers began to signal warnings of war. They swayed in splendor and radiated the majestic sovereignty of the Most High. He is my *Standard*, my *Paradigm*, and my garment revealed the insignia of the Cross.

The Helmet:

But as I took hold of my helmet, I observed that it had sustained damages. My once marvelously and intricately fashioned helmet was now dented, cracked and tarnished. I could see where the fragmented tears and cracks needed mending. For too long I allowed negative thoughts to freely meander through my mind and through this loophole my foes had been able to plant seeds of doubt, insecurities and fear.

The Holy Spirit reminded me that He would keep me in perfect peace if I kept my mind on Him. I immediately and attentively began to seize every negative thought, as commanded in **2 Corinthians 10:5** and brought it to the obedience of the Lordship of Jesus Christ. As I did this, my helmet began to shield and protect my mind from all assaults of the evil one. Every time I allowed His Word to govern my thoughts, it gave me the peace that sheltered me from the onslaughts of the adversary and shielded my mind like a powerful helmet.

I then took into account every notable and essential component of my protective covering and I discovered that one piece of weaponry stood out above all others, that is, the spiritual loin belt.

The Loin Belt:

The loin belt is a rather unusual piece of support. It is the scaffold and foundation on which all the other pieces of my arms rested; it is the bedrock where God's Truth resides. I had to allow the Word of God to have absolute dominion over my life; for the ability to use the other pieces of my armor depended on its strength and power. Therefore, it had to be grounded, established, and permanently affixed in His Truth.

If I had no loin belt, I would have no place to attach my enormous Shield or retract my Sword. I would not be able to rest my javelins or keep my breastplate from jolting in the blustering wind. My loin belt had to be thoroughly operational, and I had to be ready to take action. I had to allow the Word of God to be the operating force, for it is what held the pieces of my spiritual weaponries together. With the Word as the central and dominant role in my life and my loin belt securely fastened, I was guaranteed that all the other pieces of my gear would stay in place;

permitting me to move about with immense speed and fight with great fury.

But during the battle, I suffered agonizing heartbreak. This one was more devastating than any I had ever experienced. My heart deeply ached as I felt each dart permeate the deepest part of my soul. As I clung to the Cross, my heart fainted with fear. I lay there gasping for breath, each time as if it were my last. I needed the Savior more than ever, for the pain I carried was unbearable.

I was in trouble; I was feeble and sore broken. I moaned by reason of the disquietness of my heart. My desire was before the Lord, and my groaning was not hid from Him. My heart panted and my strength failed me. My tears were my meat night and day. I cried unto God and made a noise because of the voice of the enemy. My heart was sore pained within me, and the terrors of death fell upon me. Fearfulness and trembling came upon me, and horror, it overwhelmed and plagued me like a deadly virus

For it was not an enemy that reproached me; then I could have borne it: neither was it he that hated me that did magnify himself against me; then I would have hid myself from him. But it was a man mine equal, my guide, and my acquaintance. We took sweet counsel together and walked in the house of God in company (Psalm 38:6, 8-10, Psalm 55).

But I said I will call upon God; and the Lord shall save me, sustain me and never suffer the righteous to be moved **(Psalms 55:22)**. As I secured my *Breastplate*, it began to protect, shield, and keep me from falling apart; for the piercing wounds inflicted upon me were more detrimental than anyone could have ever imagine. But *Jehovah-Tsidkenu* was my reinforcement and He said I would be established in righteousness **(Isaiah 54:14)**.

Support for My Feet:

My feet, support and foundation were reinforced with the unyielding and immovable footing of *Jehovah-Shammah*--God's Peace. Many times the enemy endeavored to disrupt, divert, and steal my attention by causing negative events to pivot around me, but the greaves that shielded my feet protected me from being weakened and impaired. It enabled me to advance forward. Unfazed by the devil's attempts to take me down, God's prevailing Peace empowered me to maintain an inexorable march.

But not until I secured my loin belt was my faith proficiently able to douse the relentless scorching arrows that kept darting my way. Being Word-saturated and Word-soaked, my Faith Shield became dynamically empowered and a divinely impenetrable apparatus.

An immediate recollection of **Ephesians 6** then brought to mind two vital offensive artilleries of my armor - the *Sword* and *Lances* or *Prayers*. While the *Shield* protects, guards and acts as a defensive mechanism, the *Prayers* or *Lances of Prayers* work conjointly with the *Sword*.

I found the *lance* of my spiritual armor in **Ephesians 6:18**. Another word for the lance is *javelin* or *spear*, and its primary function is to cut, slice open, pierce and penetrate into the realm of the spirit. The Holy Spirit revealed that while prayer was a very essential part of my weaponry, it was the most often neglected.

Just as Roman soldiers were committed to the fighting and struggles of warfare, sword practice had to be an essential and consistent part of my preparation. The soldiers' daily stringent military maneuvers helped them develop into top-notch, incomparable opponents, and so will we if we apply ourselves.

The swords they used during practice were twice the weight of the real swords used in combat and were made of hefty and bulky timber. The soldier's mission in this exercise was to become skilled in taking advantage of his enemy. Striking and hitting him at his weakest and feeble areas in order to offset and neutralize his progress thereby reduced further advancements.

The Sword:

I had to skillfully employ the *Sword* of the Spirit much in the same way. The *logos* or written Word of God contained the guidelines and instruction I needed for my every day life, but the "*rhema*" was a specific or quickened Word from the Scriptures. It was a word given by the Holy Spirit which was placed in my heart and hands to use against the enemy. The "*rhema*" is what executed the lethal blows against my enemy causing him to recoil each time and I knew that if I was going to live to tell the tale, I had to become an expert wielder of this exclusive piece of weaponry.

My prayers became artilleries that attacked my opponent from the distance. After repenting for neglecting this very important piece of weaponry, I knew that by thrusting the *lance of my prayers and supplications* into the realm of the spirit, I was striking the enemy from a distance and I was keeping him from sneaking and attacking me close up. I also knew this would be a fight unlike any other so I made use of every form of prayer that had been made available to me just as a soldier used all kinds of lances in battle.

I faced many battles, but this fight would prove my fidelity and love to the God I said would be Lord of my life forever. Would the betrayal and loss I had just encountered push me away from Him or would I allow the heartbreak sustained draw me closer?

I held on to my *Sword* for it was the only thing that gave me support and comfort. The *Sword* had numerous components which made it an intriguing device. While it was a deadly offensive contraption during times of battle, it converted into a *Book* to provide assistance, provision and guidance during rest.

Many times I lost my way through the smog and confusion that blistered around me, causing the view of my path to become vague and formless. But the more unclear and ambiguous the journey, the more I depended on the knowledge of my *Bible* to light my path and steer me in the right direction.

The *Bible* transformed into my pillow at nights; oftentimes catching the tears that had flooded the pages of its book. The things I held closely to my heart were now replaced by this *Book* that I had come to love. It would become my companion for life.

But through trial and error, I learned to depend on the *Words* that spoke to me in the hours of my despair. When everything else failed, the promises contained in the *Book* gave me the consolation and strength I needed to go forward despite the fierce storms ahead. God was allowing the turning of the tables to strategically teach me how to competently confront my opponent head on.

Chapter 2

Reflections of a Teenage Life

I had a distorted image of what a father should be. Seeing my mother physically assaulted and battered by a man who said he loved her caused me to hate him with a pressing passion. Many times I remember thinking about taking the sword that laid next to his bed and plunging it directly into his heart. I hated him for the mental, emotional, and physical anguish he wreaked on all of us. He caused me to lose everything and everyone I loved.

My world seemed shattered for as long as I could remember. For many years, I watched as each of my five siblings left one after the other. By leaving, they were able to escape the torment they had endured for so long, but they had forgotten one very important thing, **ME**. What about **ME**? Why did everyone abandon **ME**?

Living with Papi and Mami:

I was petrified of my father. But amid the hatred and confusion I encountered, I loved him and I wanted more than anything to bring happiness to my Papi's heart. But how could I? He was so complicated and difficult to understand and he would never let anyone close enough to look into his heart.

The sound of Papi's footsteps marching upstairs for his evening bath made me altogether tremble. I always had this strange feeling that I was doing something wrong. So every evening I made sure I was found doing something good, especially when he flung open my bedroom door; if not, I knew I would be the mark of a cruel attack.

The sound of his footsteps grew louder the closer he came. What fault would he find this time? Was the shade in the window up too high or too low? Would he hit me for something that I had done or failed to do? Had he been drinking? Did he have a bad day at work? He was so unpredictable that one could never tell. The slightest thing could trigger an onslaught; so we were very careful of what we said and did.

For years, I was tormented with horrifying visions and echoes of Mami's screams. Many nights I witnessed from the staircase the corporal punishment he imposed upon her. I wondered what she had done to deserve such physical torture. Only God knew. But the psychological and emotional trauma that set in afterwards was much more damaging than anyone could ever envision.

It was an awful sight to behold the hammering of his fist that violently smash into her arms and face. Now and then he would use some funny looking silver rings that were linked together. I later found out they were brass knuckles. As he pinned her down, she struggled to break free from his evil clutches but the more she struggled to escape, the more agitated he became. Sadly, the beatings worsened; each time striking with excessive force.

I was about six years of age when I experienced the sentiments of losing someone for the first time. The second eldest sister had run away from home a week after her sweet sixteen birthday party; she was pregnant. Regrettably, in our family, running away was the only recourse. I remember the emptiness I felt when I discovered she was gone and would never return and though most of my memories of her are vague, I never forgot the love I felt in my heart towards her. There was something exceptionally special about her. Why did I always feel that I loved her more than the others? Maybe it was because she was the first one to walk out of my life.

We were scared the day she returned with her boyfriend to speak with Papi; I wondered if the young man would leave alive. I scampered to the front window and without being noticed quietly whispered a hello.

The visit reached as far as the front door and to my surprise, after some loud words, the young man left with his two feet and his head still on. Papi had disowned her and made it clear that if she ever returned to visit any of us he would kill her. From that day, we were all forbidden to ever see her or speak of her again.

Papi was usually drunk and when he wasn't, he was full of anger and much bitterness. He quarreled and complained about the things of the past and often spoke of his mother's callous love toward him. I do not recall Papi ever really being sober for long. He seemed normal but grumpy in the mornings but only when he was not recovering from a hangover. Mami would bring his coffee, and there in the bathroom he would spend the next half hour reading the New York Daily News.

On weekends, he would have already drunken approximately four to five beers by the early afternoon. I believe that his discontent with life led him to flee the inescapable and looming torment of a sober day by staying drunk and under the influence most of the time. But the frightmarish sequel of his evil cruelty would continue to haunt us for years.

The bigger and more brutal fights usually occurred during the weekends. I never really looked forward to them because he was more violent and belligerent during this time. Our drive back home from a night out was usually frightening as mother cried and yelled at him to slow down. I was surprise that he could even remember his way home.

Numerous times he'd stumble into the house only to drop to the floor like a sack of wasted potatoes. Poor Mami, she usually attempted to pick him up but he was far too heavy; she was less than five feet tall. Hence, he was left on the floor like a large dead carcass until the following morning. I often prayed that he would drown in his vomit and never wake up.

I never really knew the reason for my parents' fights but Papi never needed one. He was the king of his castle and right all the time. He was proud, a know it all, and you would never dare to correct him about anything. He was a ticking bomb most of the time and anything could trigger him off; so we made sure to stay clear and out of his way to avoid any altercations.

I remember crying alone most of the time. I do not recall ever having one person that I could confide in and share what I was really undergoing. Matter of fact, I never knew that talking to someone was an option. Choices were not a privilege that I had; Mami was a living example of that. We never verbalized our thoughts to one another, let alone to anyone else. Consequently, my emotions remained bottled up and concealed in my heart for years.

I was becoming angry and tired and not understanding or knowing where to place what I was feeling was very confusing. But miraculously, I survived the loneliness and dejection that surrounded me. I created my own world and there in the confinements of my solitude I found safety. I managed to survive but grew up very lonely, never allowing anyone close enough to see the real me. I was only existing and not living; I had no voice, no identity. Who was I? I did not know.

I recant the night he chased me for what seemed miles with a butcher knife in his hand. I was about twelve years old, and this particular night, he had been drinking excessively.

My father loved to fish, and every now and then, we would go to the river. That night, we had come to the end of the night's catch of fish and crabs and were packing up to go home. Grandmother began telling jokes as we loaded the van; she was so entertaining that night we laughed until our bellies ached.

Papi always carried an intimidating and suspicious demeanor. You would not dare whisper when he was around or laugh too hard or too much. When he heard the laughter, he made his way over to the van and belligerently swore that we had been laughing at him. I became the mark of his rage that evening and with the large knife in his hands, the chase was on. He threatened to kill me if he caught me, so of course, I ran like I never ran before. I leaped over fences and darted through people's property to escape the death that he was so readily capable of committing; I was petrified.

We did not grow up in a Christian home; but Mami did. Her father had been a deacon years ago in the church we occasionally attended as children. She had wonderful godly parents. They helped raise us for the first few years of our lives in the beautiful island of Puerto Rico. Abuela (ah-bwe-lah), my grandmother knew of the many struggles Mami encountered, but much of what happened in our home stayed in our home. Everything was a secret.

Mami upheld some of the Christian morale as she tried to give us as much of God as she knew but it was not enough to give us the solid foundation needed in knowing who Jesus Christ really was. What we needed was a consistent knowledge of the Word and a living example of true Christianity. A lack of knowledge, not being rooted in the Word of God and the suppression of an ungodly spouse made it difficult for her to grow as a child of God. His overbearing demonic influence choked any glimpse of hope she might have had. Many times she was fatally discouraged and forced into hostile oppressions of many kinds.

She lacked confidence within herself and in the ability of the God that loved her. The fear that held her captive not only delayed her liberation from spiritual, mental and emotional bondage but it also attempted to gruesomely slaughter the purpose and plan of God for her life. It also greatly hindered the probability of the success of our future.

Jesus told a story about seeds in **St. Matthew 13:20-21**. If allowed, the hardships we suffer in this present world will definitely choke any confidence we have in God. The enemy's goal is to keep us from ever seeing ourselves as God truly sees us. Poor Mami never made it to her full potential in Christ; not because it was impossible, but because she settled.

Nevertheless, when she could, she took us to church and I remember enjoying the times we went. But Papi was sure to bring a cruel end to everything and anything that gave us any contentment and peace, and eventually he stopped us from going.

But it was in that short period that the Word of God had a lasting impact on my life. The old but beautiful portrait that hung behind the church's pulpit oftentimes gave me an unusual but lovely feeling. It was so huge that it took up the entire wall, and you could not miss the words that read, "*I will never leave thee nor forsake thee; Nunca te dejare, y no te desapare.*" The words were luminously painted in a bright white that stood out against everything else and transmitted a powerful message into my heart every time. It was alive and strong and in the years to come they somehow invaded my withering soul yet, giving me a moment of solace every time I remembered them.

During the toughest times in my life those words permeate my thoughts and dreams. Since God's Word is both Spirit and Life, it had the power to whisper love and hope into my injured heart and to let me know that He was there even in the anonymity of my pandemonium and chaotic life.

But life was becoming much more difficult with each passing day. We never did anything right, and his cruel criticisms left us scarred, very discouraged and hateful toward him. The devastating words he spoke to me, *"You'll never amount to anything, you puta (slut)!"* oftentimes left me despondent and very sad. I tried really hard to remain unnoticed and avoided being in his presence as much as I could.

As a result, I faced many problems as a teenager. I struggled with low self-esteem and consequently, my school grades fell tremendously. By the age of thirteen, I ran away from home only to turn to the streets and drugs. I helped myself to whatever drugs were obtainable; for I sought anything that would haul me from the brutal realities of the hell I was living. Anything was better than the despondency I was encountering day after day, but little did I know that my father's curse of spoken words would come to settle the scores sooner than expected.

By the age of thirteen, I regarded my life as insignificant. I suffered from emotional instability, and rejection and loneliness became my companions. I had no protector, no big brother to defend me and no father to watch over me. I had no mother's gentle hugs and loving arms to run into. Adults had passed me around like a basketball while others did not want me at all. I was tired of being misunderstood, unwanted, and unloved. Was there not one person who could just love me? What had I done that had been so horrible? There were no answers to my questions.

But *Death* was ominously forthcoming and without recourse. My father's curse had given the devil the legal right to impose his vindictive treachery against me. It did not matter if I wanted to play his foul game or not; for the spoken words Papi vocalized had granted me the death warrant. It was coming to vaunt itself of its evil influence and to disseminate to the world how powerful he was.

But I was young and naive; oblivious to this ruthless game called '*life.*' I was clueless about God, His Word, and His plan for my life. The devil knew it; consequently taking advantage of my lack of knowledge and inexperience. But all was not lost, for God would not allow the devil to wipe me out before giving me my fair chance to play. My help would come at its appointed time; giving me the opportunity to take back my life, crush him and place him where he belonged—under my feet **(Romans 16:20)**; it would only be a matter of time.

Life in Tampa:

By the time I was living with my second eldest sister, I was almost fourteen years old. I admired and adored her and I wanted to be just like her. She was gorgeous, creatively fashionable and very popular among her friends. But I was deceived by the glamour of her life and I never imagined that my life would one day turn out just as empty as hers had been.

I was already doing drugs by the time I came to live with her and since my brother in-law was a drug dealer, my drug involvement deepened with each passing month. But I did not care; I was having fun as the devil made me feel like a little girl in a candy store. The drugs gave me much pleasure. I could be anyone I wanted to be and I controlled what went on in my world, so I thought. My two unwanted companions, *Rejection* and

Loneliness, dissipated with each sniff and puff, and with each exhale, I felt like I was on top of the world.

Many nights I got high with my sister, her husband and sometimes just with my friends. My brother in-law was a great guy. He was funny, warming and kind and very affectionate. He was about 4' 11" with a funny accent, and I got along with him really well.

I never remember enjoying the blessing of having my brothers. They had been stripped away from me at an early age, so I thought I was fortunate to have him take their place. He was now the male role model in my life; I felt somewhat safe.

But something evil was lurking in the shadows; something that was sure to leave me void and empty of any dignity I had left. A new vendetta of humiliation, dishonor and scorn had been forged against me; something that was sure to leave me damaged for good.

It all began the night I tried some new drugs. The effects of these drugs were quite the opposite from the others I had taken. Instead of feeling energetic and excited as usual, I was mellow, calm and relax; very relax. My sister and I both lay on the bed getting our massages. It took no time before I went into la-la land feeling totally and wonderfully blissful.

The Sexual Abuse:
Then the unexpected happened. Without warning, I felt a penetrating touch tear into me that left me instantly throbbing. My body jolted as I reacted to the awful sting. I remember trying to explain to my sister what had happened, but I was told that I had been

hallucinating from the new drug. But I knew what had just happened, and my sister beside me did not take notice to the truth of what had just occurred. She did not appeared alarmed or concern because she was too high and lost in her own world.

As time elapsed, I became uncomfortable and edgy, for his aberrant touches were no longer accidents but deliberate, planned and intentional. They had become a normal habit for him. Many times his arms stroked across my breast when reaching for something or his body unexpectedly collided into mine as I turned a corner or came out of a room.

As a result, I went into a mental shut down and my level of drug use perpetuated much deeper. I pretended that nothing ever happened. I convinced myself that it would soon all go away, and in time it did. I never spoke about it or mentioned it to anyone. Why should I? There was no one to protect me anyway.

I did not consider him an evil or a bad person but I was a bit more cautious around him. I did not understand his sudden interest because I was young and vulnerable and could not make sense of his cunning advances. Nevertheless, I enjoyed getting high as much as I could as I continued my routine of getting wasted on drugs for days.

But my life of party and having a good time finally came to a crashing end when my sister left for New York for several days and left me with her husband and two children. One dreadful morning after partying all night, I was awakened to find him on me; touching me in places that were reserved as private. I was perplexed and confused, and although weak and groggy as a result of the withdrawals, I managed to shove him away from me. I went ballistic; throwing anything my hands got hold of at him. His attempt to calm me down only made the situation worst. I then ran into the kitchen and grabbed a knife. The rage I felt possessed me as I viciously swung at him.

His friend entered during the fight and straight away tackled me; during the scuffle, the knife fell out of my hands. Together they pinned me against the wall and my brother in-law's nonchalant look conveyed that he had done nothing wrong and that I had over reacted. I left them picking up shattered pieces of mirror as I walked out the door with a bag of clothes claiming never to return.

My way of escape was made clear but now I had nowhere to lodge. I found an empty dilapidated apartment within the complex and there I decided to lay my head. Two of my friends decided to join me that night.

We planned the events for that evening and they brought sleeping bags, munchies and music. But our limited supply of drugs soon led us to plan a break-in at my sister's house to steal the drugs that were hidden in her laundry basket.

During our euphoric festivity, I was spaced-out and did not mind that I had taken lodge in the abandoned apartment that was corroded and dirty. Nothing else really mattered because here, no one could hurt me. I was satisfied with my life of getting high and being with my friends; it was my only escape from reality.

But tragedy would be the result of this evening's affair because my sister had returned from her trip that night, and she was looking for me. Someone had snitched and revealed my hidey-hole. I could see the look of disappointment and disgust on her face when she stepped into the room. She grabbed me by my hair and neck, smacked me a time or two, and dragged me home. She was irate and I couldn't blame her. I had yet to know that what I had stolen was about two thousands dollars worth of drugs.

My sister immediately contacted my mother and explained that she could longer keep me. I was being sent home at once. Panic instantly set in, for I knew I was in trouble. I quickly began to plan my way of escape and I had to think fast because there was no way I was going back to my father's house. Death was better than going back.

I slipped into the bathroom before anyone could notice. I could hear the continual yelling and arguing between my sister and her husband outside the bathroom walls. It reminded me of when my parents fought. I wanted it to stop. I wanted the screaming, the yelling and the pain that had now overtaken me to cease.

But the seething fires of grief and sorrow had found me once again; this time hurling unfathomable billows of darkness my way. With it they carried shackles, and their brutal vapors linked themselves to my aching heart. There was no relief from the dejection I now faced. I needed a final escape from the unremitting torture that stalked me.

The Lure of Suicide:
It would be only a matter of time before they found me

again, and by now I was tired of running, hiding and fighting for my life. Hopelessness and helplessness molested me until I was deadened and unfeeling and the voices outside the bathroom walls eventually faded. Suicide wasted no time to voice her conniving verdict and her deviously poetical librettos relentlessly echoed in my head. The more I rehearsed the words I heard, the more I became ensnared by its persuasive deception. Its convincing and treacherous invitation lured me toward the closet adjacent to the bathroom where I stood that night. I quickly gathered the bottles of pills from off the medicine shelf and laid them on the bathroom counter. As I gazed into the mirror, all I could see was a pitiful little girl who had tried desperately to be loved and accepted. Why had no one loved me enough to call me their own?

Loneliness mercilessly joined in full force to plunge its stinging twinge that filtered right through the center of my soul; this time ripping and shredding me like a hungry predator would his prey. Desperate to bring an end to their cruel and inexhaustible attack of criticism and condemnation, I took one last look into the mirror and irately exclaimed, *"I hate you!"*

My heart brusquely palpitated as I shoved handful of pills into my mouth; for I knew not how death would seize me. Would it come slowly or quickly? I was scared because I knew my death was going to be excruciatingly painful. I had consumed cocaine, speed, alcohol, and marijuana within the hour, and the combined substances was going to chaos in my system. But nothing mattered at this point. Enduring the physical pain temporarily was no match to the unending and inexorable inner wounds I had carried for years.

That night I was sent to stay with my cousin and his wife. As I was going home with them, I remember thinking about what I had done. While I had no regrets, I wearyingly waited to see what would happen.

As the sleeping arrangements was all set, I took my blanket and crawled into bed. But it was very difficult to sleep, as time stood still that night. I heard the stroke of each tick and the cadence of every tock. I cannot remember how much time had elapsed, but I knew that the big bang of my midnight hour was approaching; the moment that death would snatch me into eternal darkness. This would be the longest night of my life.

But just like a tsunami that strikes the shorelines without warning, I was hit with immense blusters of pain that left me breathless. It felt as if someone or something was ferociously and violently shredding my insides. My internal organs went into ruthless convulsions from the overdose. As I tried to bellow for help, I was unable to because the pain worsened with each passing second. The intensity of the throbbing spasms made it difficult for air to flow into my lungs, incapacitating my speech and movement. It felt like an eternity before I could catch my next breath.

By now, little strength remained. I knew that it was only a matter of time before I would pass out and die. So with one last might and a desire to live, I succeeded to bellow a thunderous and piercing cry. Alarmed by the shriek that echoed through the house, my cousins scurried over to my bedside. I was found slouched over the bed holding my belly. They kept asking what the matter was, but I could not gather enough air into my lungs to speak. I was hurting terribly but somehow succeeded at mumbling, *"Pills, took pills."*

I was vomiting profusely and feeling cold by the time I was brought through the emergency room. I knew I was dying, but I remember praying to God in my mind. I told him that I was sorry, and if I survived, I would never attempt anything like it again.

I was rushed through the corridors as doctors and nurses surrounded my bed. Everyone was talking and moving about rather quickly; speaking in lingoes I did not understand. My stomach needing pumping and every second counted; for the amount of chemicals I consumed was proving fatal by the minute.

By now I was deliriously irrational, pulling and tugging at the tubes they had inserted up my nose and throat and yanking out my IV's. As the poison engrossed my system, I fell into a state of shock, and from that point everything darkened.

I was disoriented when I woke up the following morning. Even today, just about everything that went on during my recovery remains a blur. I do remember Mami in the hospital room and doctors psychologically probing and analyzing me; asking questions as to why I had tried to take my life. But I could not tell them the truth about the facts that led up to my suicide attempt. I was told not to tell. I kept it to myself and my life went on.

Eventually, any dreams I had left faded away like smoke rings in thin air. The miasma of dejection repeatedly darkened my fate as I was left with an uninviting fog that left me empty each time; never becoming more than what my father said I would be.

Back at My Father's House:

But Children's Protective Services (CPS) was now involved, and I was being sent to live with my parents once again. This time I was scared to death. No sibling had ever run away from home and returned. What would become of me? Only time would tell.

The next several days were quiet around the house; maybe because we were being monitored by CPS and my father knew to play it safe. But one evening, surprisingly, Papi began to make conversation; he wept as he told me how much he loved me. This was the first time in my life I had ever heard my father say I love you, and it was the first time I had ever seen him cry too.

But the recollection of my father's state of brokenness would be my last. From that day, I never again saw him contrite or remorseful about anything, and in no time he was back to his wicked ways. Constant abuse and violence seemed to be his only nature and I never understood what caused him to switch to anger and violence so quickly.

Papi had quit school at an early age to work and Mami was only fifteen years of age when he ran away with her. They had moved from Puerto Rico to New York in the forties, and like most immigrants, they had no choice but to settle for mediocre jobs. Life had proven to be difficult, especially without an education. Mami worked as a seamstress in a factory while Papi became head-Forman in a welding company.

His childhood memories were very unhappy ones. I do not think he was ever truly loved by his mother. His father had died when he was about twelve years old, and by the way he spoke about him, I knew he loved him very much. But resentment and hostility emanated from his heart when he spoke about his mother's maltreatment of him. It was evident that she had played favorites with the children.

With the type of upbringing and childhood he had, it was impossible to believe that he could give or do any better. His only male role model had died and the result of his loss was devastating. The only person in his life that seemed to truly love him had died and he was left with a mother that had never hugged him or told him she loved him.

The evil words he spoke over us were a mere reflection of what his mother had done to him, and because hurting people hurt people, the pattern of the curse had fallen on us. Papi could not give to us what he himself never had. That curse of the mental, emotional, and physical abuse could only be broken by the power of the *Divine Exchange* that has been made available to us when Jesus died on the Cross.

A Teenage Runaway:

I lasted at home no more than two weeks. His indecent verbal jargon caused me to become very depressed. The emotional mutilation of my self-confidence diminished little by little, leaving a scarring and bruising that no therapy or medicine could ever heal. The enemy was making certain that I was damaged goods before I had my fair chance in life. I had been battered emotionally and physically for so long that my self-esteem had been desecrated to the point of no return. My father accomplished an excellent job at fulfilling the devil's assignment. He received an A+ and was placed on the devil's honor roll.

As time passed, my parents became Jehovah-Witnesses and were having weekly studies in our home. My mother grew up in a born-again Christian home in Puerto Rico, but somewhere along life's way, she lost the fundamental teachings of Christianity. Easily deceived by this cultic doctrine, it began to infiltrate our home. Jehovah Witnesses were committed to their cause but the teachings did not contain the resurrection power needed to make a life changing impact on my father's life; for only the Living Word which is Jesus Christ possesses the power to make such a change. Only the power of the *Cross* can turn a man from his wicked ways and change him into something he has never been.

It was during a Jehovah-Witness study night that I planned my second escape. I knew this one would be for good, for I vowed never to return to my parent's home; I'd rather sleep under cardboard with the homeless than to live there.

That evening while they studied in the dining room, I returned to my bedroom and quickly locked the door behind me. I could feel my hands shaking from fear. My father would skin me alive if I was caught, so this escape had to be quick and efficient; there would be no room for mistakes. I turn on my music, speedily packed my belongings, broke the screen and crawled out through my bedroom window.

I was very afraid as my friends waited for me in the getaway car. I tracked it down the long Florida road that night and when I took one look behind me, I found that my shoes had fallen from a hole in the plastic bag. I felt like Hansel & Gretel, only instead of leaving bread trails, I was dropping crumbs of shoes; I ran back to get them.

As you can imagine, my school days were over, but I was not complaining; I had become totally disinterested with school. I was now considered an official high school dropout. This pattern had circled all the way down the family tree and I was its next victim.

They called the authorities and I was declared a legal teenage runaway. I stayed low for a while living with my teenage boyfriend and his father. Though we shared the same room and the same bed, I did not do the things that my teenage girlfriends were doing with their boyfriends. I was too scared; nevertheless, he was a good friend and his father was trying to help.

But I eventually ruined the relationship when I went to a party. I met some new people that night who offered dope and naturally, I wanted to go with the harder drugs. The beer, Jack Daniels and shots of vodka were not really my style. It was only when I had no drugs that I would turn to drinking. I left the party only to have a very bad and sickening experience; the stuff had been cut with heroine and speed balls which made me very ill.

I was so hammered that night that I could not remember my address or my way home. When I finally did get home the next morning, my luggage was packed and on the front porch. With nowhere else to go, I ended up tapping on the back window of my girlfriend's home. There in her bedroom closet, I hid for long periods. I was given food and water and I only came out when her mother went off to work.

The closet sounded like a good idea at the time; it was fun and exciting being hidden and getting away with it. But it wasn't too long before I really understood my unpromising condition and when the closet became uncomfortable, the remainder of my days was spent in the back of her uncle's car.

Unnoticed by anyone, I continued my routine of sleeping in the car and took baths and ate at my friend's house while her mother was away. Ultimately, we both knew that we could no longer continue our little hide and seek game. There were too many close calls as her mom would sometimes barge into the bedroom unannounced. We knew it would only be a matter of time before we got caught.

My life continued with many teenage misadventures involving many uncertainties and risks. I was placed in foster homes and juvenile centers. I became a victim of sodomy and suffered under the evil hands of molestation and rape.

Chapter 3

Words Can Never Hurt Me…
or Can They?

The Word of God is very clear about the power of words. Proverbs 18:21 tells us that death and life are in the power of what we say; that is how potent words really are. They are powerfully persuasive in that they are able to exert or capable of exerting great influence.

Hitler's vendetta against the Jews is a prime example. By the power of his words, he was able to influence and move an entire nation into believing in race superiority and the importance of race purification. He did this by "politicking" his opinions, theory and philosophy through vainglorious words.

Still today, many of us do not detect the enemy wreaking havoc in our lives through our negative and faithless words. Remember the old saying, sticks and stones may break my bones, but WORDS can never hurt me? How wrong they are; for words can and will hurt.

The Power of Words:
Words are the creative life force of everything. God himself set this example from the beginning of time. **Genesis 1:3** says that God said, "Let there be…," and there was. In view of the fact that we are created in the image and likeness of God, and since we are His children, then we must also conclude that we have the same creative power to act just like Him. Our words have the ability to affect our future and the people and things we govern. The curse of failure that followed me

was the harvest of what my father had sown through his faithless and negative words. I was guaranteed complete failure all due to the principle of the death and life in the tongue law.

Words can have a strong physiological effect that can produce a powerful effect on the body or mind. Hitler became successful at accomplishing his goals by putting a plan of action in operation. Though his goals were evil and corrupt, he caused others to buy into his deception through propaganda and false indoctrination. Sometimes, I wonder how an entire nation of people could become infected with such corruptness. But he poisoned their minds to believe they were a powerful people who were superior to all others. His prompting of self-righteousness and pride emasculated, weakened and demoralized their intelligence and blinded their competence to what was morally correct.

Words are also strong and effective in producing great emotional and physical reactions. Hitler targeted the pride of man by using intimidation and fear to seize and commandeer their will, thoughts and emotions. The outcome and end result of Hitler's persuasive campaigning crusade of self-pride and hate was the massacre and murder of millions and millions of the Jewish people. As we can see, this type of negativity which began in the mind of one person gradually infiltrated the hearts and mind of what I believe were once good people.

Words are very much like seeds; they produce after their kind. Negative words are dormant; alive but not active. They are undeveloped and hidden for a season and are only activated when verbalized through human articulation. The spoken word is the life creating force it needs to generate, discharge, and set off the negative or positive results in our lives.

The Damages of Negative Words:

When negative words are spoken to a child, it will spawn negative results in his life. Think of the child that has been told all his life that he was bad, ugly and stupid. The words or seeds spoken will produce instability, insecurities, doubts and fears over a period of time; consequently affecting many areas of his life. The probability exists that he may face one to several complications in his self-esteem, relationships with others, while suffering from mental and emotional instabilities all because of what was said or done to him.

Have you ever faced a problem you were not sure you would overcome? Did the power of an encouraging word from a friend, pastor or teacher make a difference? Most of us will answer yes. Why? Because it was the power in the positive words that enabled us to rethink and reconsider the risk and the probability. Positive words produce good fruit; negative words spawn rotten outgrowth.

The words my father had spoken created the life it needed to legally propagate the result of a troubled future, and now it was only a matter of time before they would come to settle the score. My father had cursed me with his own lips.

Chapter 4

Brooklyn, My Spiritual Egypt

After traveling for approximately one year in 1983, I made my way for "The Big Apple" —the great New York City! It was about three o'clock in the afternoon when the Greyhound bus entered the city limits. I was excited yet worried about how I would survive in "The Big Apple."

My ten months of traveling from state to state selling an all purpose cleaner finally came to a cruel end when the big boss realized he couldn't score. I had no plan of action and no one knew I was coming. I was in Columbus, Ohio when I got fired so I decided to head home - New York.

I observed the humongous buildings along the way and every one of them seemed to tell a story. As we passed, they silently echoed their tales of prideful triumphs while others of crushing defeat. There were pretty ones, ugly ones, intricately sophisticated ones and really dirty, run-down and dilapidated ones. It was an amazing sight and their diversity exuded an ambiance of vibes and grooves for the poor and rich, black and white and everything else in between. Although New York was an amazing place to be, the flamboyant lights and creative structures could not compare to my convoluted problems that were sky rising.

My Encounter with Prominence:
It was that summer afternoon, in the famous Penn Station that I met a young man whom I will name

"*Prominence.*" If you look around today, you can still find him hanging out on the corners of "*Rebellion Street*" and "*Delusion Boulevard*" of every city.

Prominence is a very well known but arrogant legend. From his cathedra flows infamy and unhealthy ideologies. He stems from the root of *Pride* and can be found in the atrocious dumps of drug infested places to the polished palaces in the uttermost parts of the world. His exaggerated view of self-importance is warped and inconceivably perverted.

While his job requirements are many-sided, it is very specific in nature. His primary targets are the abandoned and abused young ones. Children who received little to no validation or affirmation from their parents become the object of his corrupt and immoral affection. He lures you with his articulated speech that is filled with fallacious kindness and deadly poison; nothing wholesome can be found in him.

He feeds on the degradation of your past, and his strength totally depends on your inability to recognize your true value. His relentless pursuit of wounded females that possess elevated levels of deficiency in self-worth satisfies his untamed hunger until you become the mark of his cruel abusive language and the tormented victim of his never-ending mercy.

Once ensnared, you are quickly dragged into the melancholic sludge of your depression; finally, you are yoked and quelled into a chagrined state of unavoidable disconsolation.

Prominence's Mother—Supercilious:

One of his mother's names is "*Supercilious*." She is the part of you that lurks silently in the background of your mind, that is, until the rise of the titan. When the stage lights are on her, she wastes no time to perform her gaudy cabaret. Her exhibition can be found entertaining by others quite like her.

Her greatest enemy is *The Consuls*. Though she is able to exert considerable force, she lacks the capability of being emotionally resilient in a positive way. Needless to say, she is uncultivated and unrestrained; her traditions will always pilot you off-course because she never takes advice. She is bossy, quick tempered, ill-mannered and vastly unpolished.

You must be careful when dealing with *Supercilious*, for she is ruthless and contemptuously indifferent; she is filled with hate and awfully condescending. She is without doubt disloyal and won't give it a second thought to abandon you in your greatest hour of need. You do not want her as your companion.

By the time *Prominence* and *Supercilious* are finished with you, you are left alone to waste away, craving and seeking for love in all the wrong places. You become desperate just like the drug addict, always needing that quick fix.

My enemy knew me all too well and could not wait to further lead me into his web of deception. He was aware of the scars of disdain and emptiness I carried over the years. Oh, how I longed for love. I yearned for it; for once in my life, I wanted to know what it would feel like to be the center of someone's world.

As he did his notorious smooth talking, his quite frequent compliments caused me to blush. I had never been told that I was beautiful so much in one day. What did he see? Was I really that pretty? When I looked into the mirror, all I could see was failure, complete failure. But here he was telling me all the things I had longed to hear.

The words he spoke that afternoon uplifted me in a way I had never experienced before. I could sense the pride brewing on the inside; something I do not recall ever feeling. The effects were like taking drugs for the first time and I was feeling really good.

With the right words to say, it did not take much flattery to captivate my parched and fading soul. And so, my compliant and spellbound spirit was easily hoodwinked as he somehow convinced me that I could get a career in modeling and dancing. With the body of a dancer and a pretty face, I could earn lots of money. I took his card and told him I would consider it.

But getting to New York was not the biggest problem I faced, finding a place to live was. It had only been a year and a half earlier since I resided with my sister. She was the third eldest and a good sister as far as I can remember. But being young and married just a little over two years and with two young toddlers, let's just say she could no longer withstand the issues of dealing with a troubled teenager.

I was always into fights; I think my height made me an easy target for others to pick on. But I was my father's child and many times others got more than they bargained. I fought with such rage that I was able to defeat girls twice my height and weight. In fact, my height was my greatest advantage; I could move like a butterfly and sting like a bee. Needless to say, fighting did not get me anywhere but kicked out in the third week of school. I remember that fight, it took three security officers to get me off the girl that day.

But here I was once again, never having a steady place to call home. I was a survivor and I'd make it somehow. As I made my telephone call from the Penn station, my eldest sister decided to take me in. This sister is the sweetest and humblest of all sisters. I have seen many of her struggles; many of which were grave. But I was also able to witness her ability to make the best in every situation.

Life was good the first few weeks. I made many friends in the neighborhood and for a while, things seemed quite normal. Then it was time to look for a job. Since I did not want to go back to school, I had to find work so that I could help.

I was only fifteen and my experiences were very limited. Without a high school diploma, I had to settle for mediocre jobs with cheap paying salaries. I found many positions available as a sales clerk on one of East New York's biggest shopping region but I was dissatisfied with each place of employment. About every two months, I would quit and move to another store in hopes that the next storeowner wasn't a dirty sexual pervert looking for a quick fix. After several months, I decided it was time give *Prominence* a call.

He was glad to hear from me and wondered why it had taken me so long to call. We decided that we would meet up in the city to further discuss the details of my new job. After agreeing that he would get sixty percent of whatever I made, I was ready for my first show in a New Jersey nightclub. As I watched the girls seductively danced the night away, I made some quick notes and determined that I could do it.

As my turn approached, I took a deep breath and made my way onto the stage. I knew how to dance; so I moved my flesh in motion to the sound of each beat. With the thunderous music vigorously pounding and with the sporadic movement of the lights, I fell into a trance. Feeling like a superstar, I became lost with the resonance and pulsation of each tempo; seductively and passionately swinging my body. I was at the top of the world when I was on stage; an idol of beauty to behold.

Top dancers from other night clubs were brought in to perform weekly. She would perform a dance or two and when it was time to leave, she was escorted by some flashy and glitzy guy into a limousine that waited outside. I was very naive to the schematics of this business. But in the new world I was encountering, I wanted everyone to remember me just like the dancers that came and left unforgettable impressions. What would it take and what would I need to do to reach that fame?

The club owners knew I was only fifteen and did not want to risk the possibility of having their licensed revoked so I was restricted from the bar. But I managed to stay afloat by getting my own stuff to keep me high. Eventually, it did not take long before the demands of changing into skimpier outfits and exposing body parts became an issue. It was a dirty business and if you were pretty, the other girls weren't as friendly. But it was a competition and I could hold my own.

I came from a lineage of fighters; my father was a ruthless boxer and the Don Juan of his day. I remember growing up in Bedford Stuyvesant where he was much respected. No one ever bothered Mr. Martinez or his family. They knew he wouldn't think twice to pop you; needless to say the fruit didn't fall far from its tree.

The first time I held a gun in my hands, I was about fourteen years old. A friend and I had driven to a local neighborhood to buy some marijuana. But I made a huge mistake when I turned over the money before receiving the goods. The guy took off with my money never to be seen again. As we drove around looking for him, I felt powerful with the gun in my hands. I was so angry that I probably would have shot him if I saw him.

The Beginning of the Dreams:

Over the next few weeks, I kept having odd dreams and my life was becoming uncomfortable and edgy again. I was familiar with the routine and knew that I'd be found by these treacherous and evil rabble-rousers that had made my life a living hell since I can remember. How much longer could I run?

My dreams bothered me, and I somehow knew in my heart that God was calling me. Something was heavily brewing on the inside of me. In the city of my soul was a cry for a God I did not know. But how could this be? I had not known Him or His ways. It was Spirit calling unto spirit; deep calling unto deep **(Psalms 42:7).**

Dream 1:

The first dream I had, I was alone on a deserted and dry flatland. There were no buildings or houses, no trees or breeze blowing, and no signs of life; I could see the perimeters of the ends of the earth all around me, and everything was very dry. When I looked up into the heavens, a square or window shaped took form, and the biggest hand I had ever seen came forth. I did not feel threatened or scared as the hand stretched out towards me and in response, I stretched out my hand to the hand—God's hand! I was awakened knowing that the Spirit of God was calling.

Dream 2:

The second dream I had was of the Holy Spirit upon me and I was speaking in tongues **(Acts 2:11, Acts 19:6).** Again, I was awakened with a revelation that the Lord was calling me.

There is something birthed in man that is given only by God Himself and that is the breath of life. It wasn't until God breathed into man's nostril that he became a living soul **(Genesis 2:7).** It was my spirit that knew to cry out to its Maker. My reservoirs of life had been filled with false hope and empty promises; it had been like trying to fit a circle into a square; it just didn't fit. My longing and thirsting could only be filled by God.

My Quest for God and the Homeless Times:

As I began my quest for a God I did not know my life was instantly hit by a whirlwind that turbulently caused my life to fall further apart. I was innocently kicked out of my sister's home by her perverted and lustful husband after she returned from a trip. I finally understood my father's disapproval of him. He was a lazy pothead who enjoyed nothing more than watching pornography and getting high all day. If my Papi did not understand anything else, he understood the evil ways of a man. All he wanted was for her to have a good husband who would work to take care of his wife and children; he was the complete opposite. What was it about these licentious and immoral brother in-laws?

I ended up homeless and on the streets of East New York. Getting high every night became my way of life. Friends took turns staying up with me until there were not enough friends for each day of the week. One night after attempting to sleep on the back steps of an old Catholic church, an overwhelming gloominess swept over me. I finally realized how alone I was with no one to talk to and nowhere else to go. I had suffered days of being tired, hungry and I needed a bath. I felt so lost.

In desperate need of sleep, I walked into the building I had formerly lived in and made my way to the roof. I thought I would try to rest there but had become terrified that someone could possibly throw me over while I slept so I parked myself away from the roof's edge.

As I was lost in thought over the way my life had turned out, I began to weep. There was no way out of this lifestyle and no one would help. I needed to be rescued but no one cared enough to come. In desperation, I fell to my knees and looked up to the heavens. It was in that moment of despair and my eyes bursting with tears that I cried unto a God I had only heard about. I cried, **"If you're the God you say you are; if you're the God you claim to be, you see where I am, help me!"** As I knelt there sobbing for a while, I thought that if anyone had been looking out of their window, they would have surely thought I was crazy and strung out on drugs.

"Rescued" by a Drug Dealer:

My final days of sleeping outdoors would soon come to end when a New York-New Jersey drug dealer took me into his home. I met him through a mutual friend and he appeared sincere in his interest to help. I remember when I got into his sports car for the first time. I told him that for over a week I had been living in the street and was in dire need of a helping hand, but if he had any motives other than helping me he could forget it because I wasn't interested. I was ready to step out of the car when he said expressed that he wanted to help.

He took me to his home and I found great relief that his aunt and uncle lived there; I felt safer with them there. He made plans to have me enrolled in school and provided my basic needs. I was introduced to some of his family and friends and we went out a lot.

But the fact that I was only fifteen and he was a lot older did not stop him from trying to score when he could. But I knew how to handle guys like him and initially, I was far from any threats. Telling him no every time and sticking to it finally made him stop his advancements toward me. However, it was only after he became controlling and told me that he had fallen in love me and wanted to marry me that things became a bit doubtful. I was well schooled on obsessive men and their ability to kill you if they couldn't have you and I wasn't ready to die; at least not yet.

After months of heavy drug use, traveling in fast cars, and staying in cottage houses on the beach near the boardwalks in Wildwood, New Jersey, I was still unfulfilled and empty. I wanted something more meaningful for my life; just never knew where to begin.

I knew I was trapped again and now my life had become an everyday gamble; with moments of never knowing what card would be played on me. I kept a watchful eye and took life one day at a time.

God's Angel of Mercy:

But one day, I was led to visit an old favorite fifth grade teacher of mine, Ms. Grant. She was a Christian and the former teacher of my brother just before me. Growing up, I had the privilege of attending her little Bible classes that she occasionally held in her home. Although my visits were only two or three, they were enough for the Seeds of Life to be sown into my heart.

As I entered her classroom, she welcomed me with a warm smile. I was overtaken by the delightful reception she conveyed as she beckoned me to sit in a small chair nearby. While I gazed around the classroom, I was reminded of my former years in the same room that appeared rather small now. I fixed my eyes where I sat when I was in her class. I thought how life was so different now.

As we began to make small talk, I stared into her lovely eyes that were always hidden behind what I thought to be the ugliest glasses. I always thought they were too big for her face, but she was stunningly beautiful even with the big glasses.

Overwhelmed by my situation and needing someone to talk to, I wasted no time to tell her my depressing saga. As I emptied my heart before her, I took comfort knowing that she patiently listened. As I spoke, her facial expressions conveyed concern and unbelief.

When I had given a full account of my life, the look in her big eyes communicated nothing but love and compassion. Straight away she insisted that we go to the house and pack my belongings to get away. She quickly finished her last minute classroom chores and we scuttled outside and into her car.

Upon approaching the heavily drug infested area, I could feel a dark sensation sweeping over me. Though everything was happening rather quickly, I knew this was an opportunity I would not let slip by. I seized the moment by making a decision that would change the course of my life forever.

As my opportunity to escape the hell I was living presented itself, I still had to contend with the fear that was growing like yeast. What if he came home and found me packing? What would he say, or worse, what would he do? I was so scared, you could hear my heart pounding a mile away. I grew intensely nervous as I scamper throughout the house gathering my belongings. As I searched through the dresser drawers, I grabbed what I could and chucked whatever would fit into my suitcase.

As I made my way back to the car, I had a strong feeling that I had just been rescued from the clutches of something evil. I was more than relieved and it was as if a load had rolled off my back. But the question I asked myself was, "What now?" What turn of events would unfold for my life; for it had been a cycle of traveling from place to place and living like a nomad and a wanderer with no hope and no future. Why should I believe that this trip would be any different?

Chapter 5

The Godmother

But little did I know that *Heaven's Counsel* held a scheduled appointment on my behalf... I stayed two days with my other sister while Ms. Grant called a woman's meeting to order. Obviously, I was the subject matter to be discussed and unknown to me, my ill-fated dilemma was to be presented to a team of God-fearing women. Thank God for these women because they had a love and a desire to serve God. It was obvious by the turn out on "a last minute call for duty" on my behalf.

The first test of faith for these women came during prayer, when asked who would be willing to make the sacrifice to take me into their home and provide mentorship and discipleship. A Trinidadian woman would later testify that during the prayer, three times she heard the Spirit of the Lord say, *"You take her,"* and in obedience to the voice of the Lord, she raised her Pentecostal finger and graciously said, *"I'll take the young girl."*

Without delay, arrangements were made for me to be placed in her home and two days later we were on the FDR Drive heading to the Bronx. As I took my luggage that had been my companions as I traveled all over the south coast, they looked tired and worn, just as I had been. Why should this trip be any different, I thought to myself? But I never realized that this journey would be the beginning of my mark on history's Biblical timeline.

As we approached our destination, I knew I was in a predominant Latin neighborhood. You could hear the loud shrieks of people talking and laughing and the unbearable sounds of Latin music that ricocheted from every direction. As we entered the apartment building, we were greeted by the aromas of the different ethnic foods that had traveled down the hallways and into the lobby.

When they rang the doorbell, I nervously waited to see who was on the other side. Would I like the family? Would they like me? What were they like? Where they nice or mean? Clean folks or slobs? Were they Hispanics or blacks? My mind was flooded with a million thoughts as it felt like a lifetime before the door opened.

To my surprise, when the door finally opened, a strikingly beautiful Trinidadian woman greeted us with an engaging hello. She had lengthy black hair and high cheekbones. Her smile was the most becoming because there was an inner beauty that exuded every time she smiled. Right behind her was not one, not two, not even three, but four anxious children readily waiting in line to greet their new house guest. There were three boys that ranged from ages eight to eleven and a little girl that was five. Their beaming eyes were full of excitement as they each introduced themselves.

From the moment I stepped into the apartment, I could sense a loving ambiance flowing in the air; it seemed to dominate the home. I was taken to my sleeping quarter which was in the living room, and to the corner was a nicely made up bed. As I sat down, the children all sat on the couch across from me. They seemed very eager and curious to know all about me.

I quickly observed that there was no husband or father; but for a single mother of four, I thought this woman had done exceptionally well. The children were in order and very well mannered. Her sociable and affable ways made it easy for me to relax. They appeared to be a very sweet and loving family and we bonded immediately.

Our relationship began to quickly blossom but no sooner did she find herself facing the challenging issues that go hand in hand with rebellious teenagers. My defiant attitude was the second test she would have to vie with. Would she have the stamina to go head to head with me or would she like everyone else give up and quit?

But the Holy Spirit had given her the strategy and the plan that would outwit Satan's most intelligent demonic being. Many times the Lord will lead us to do things that will go against the grain. Our "proselytic" views make us believe that everything will be a smooth sail but when things go wrong as they sometimes will we become discouraged and question whether we really heard from the Lord in the first place.

Confidence and trust in our Savior is an essential part of the believer's walk. Our spiritual senses must develop over the years so that we can discern His voice. We must be apt to follow His directions to the utmost. If we don't, then we risk the likelihood of failing at the mission at hand causing much chaos.

Peter confirmed this truth when he asked Jesus if he could walk on water with him; an act that goes against men's wisdom and definitely the laws of nature. But it was under the direct influence of Jesus that he was commanded to walk. Peter walked on water until he allowed the diverse changes of his surroundings to speak over and against what he was first instructed to do **(Matthew 14:29-30)**.

In a similar way, this woman was taking a risk. She was a single woman with four children and taking in a teenage girl with the issues I had was a real threat. I smoked, did drugs, and was somewhat promiscuous; so realistically, she was risking the odds of the negative influences I could possibly impose upon her children. But threat or no threat, and against all the odds, the only thing she had to bank on was the fact that she knew she had heard from the Lord.

The first time she realized that we were heading for problems was when I refused to go to church with her. I told her that I did not go to church on Tuesdays. But she was the least discouraged, for she was a praying woman; it seemed like every time I saw her she was praying. Friday evening came and I declined again, refusing to go to youth night and giving her the same excuse. She skipped her Saturday choir rehearsal because I was adamant about not going to church, but I promised that I would go with her and the children that Sunday.

She did not harass or made me feel uncomfortable in any way. She did not demonstrate signs of bitterness or anger at the fact that I had refused to go to church all week or because she had to miss choir rehearsal; something that she enjoyed and looked forward to every weekend.

There is something much more important awaiting us when we patiently wait for the promise of the Father. We can become discouraged when things do not go exactly the way we think they should. But if we can remember that when the Lord asks us to do something then we ought to trust Him every step of the way. We must never forget **Proverbs 3:5-6: "Trust in the Lord**

with all thine heart and lean not unto thine own understanding. In all thy ways acknowledge him and he shall direct thy paths." Her obedience to follow God's plan would pay off with great dividends.

Chapter 6

The Cross and the Caterpillar

I woke up anxious yet excited about attending church Sunday morning. I knew exactly what I was going to wear. I pulled out the only white dress I had along with a red belt, red pumps, red purse and some matching red earrings. I looked like a candy cane fully decked in red and white, but I felt confident.

When we got outside, I was embarrassed as the driver pulled up in a funny looking, ugly yellow church bus. It looked like a bus that was used for transporting the mentally retarded and I thought they had to be kidding if they thought I was going to get in. But there were other passengers aboard and to avoid a scene or embarrassing anyone, I bit the bullet and stepped in.

The people on the bus seemed super friendly, surprised and very excited to meet me. My new mother had not mentioned my existence to anyone until that day. I was pleasantly surprised as she introduced me as her daughter; it gave me an immediate sense of belonging.

It wasn't long before we pulled up in front of a little store front church; its front doors were wide open you could see straight inside. As I entered, I was greeted by an usher who gave me a very hospital welcome. On my way down the isle, there were people to my left and people to my right and they all transmitted the same delightful smile the greeters gave. Their greetings were heartfelt salutations and I sensed a wonderful presence in the air; a peace unlike anything I had ever experienced before. I was glad I came.

The praise and worship was awesome. They sang songs of redemption and victory and danced with joyful liberation; something I knew absolutely nothing about but I joined in anyway. The music was especially inviting and I was savoring every bit of it. They had a full blown band of energetic musicians. Their music was especially different from anything that I had ever heard. The people were primarily from the island of Jamaica and it was their custom to worship the way they did back home. I heard traditional hymns sung in reggae and calypso rhythms and I loved it.

But something major began to take place in my heart as the man of God spoke. My insignificant little life had somehow found its way into his message. I felt like an open book as he read the pages of my troubled past. This man knew nothing about me, yet there he was preaching my life as if he had been a fly on my wall all along. I hung on every word, every sound, and every syllable spoken. He had my undivided attention that by the time he reached the end of his sermon, I felt like running to the altar.

An Invitation to Receive Jesus:

The invitation to accept Jesus was made, and I wanted with everything to raise my hand and shout I want Him, I need Him. Like the woman of Samaria, I was thirsty and I wanted Jesus to quench my desiccated soul. I knew that Jesus would change my life and give me hope; He was what I had been searching for all along. He would forever eradicate the clouds of emptiness and loneliness that had hovered over my life for years.

My heart melted as the people softly sang *Jesus, Jesus, Jesus, there is something about that name.* But just before I could raise my hand to indicate that I wanted this Jesus, the devil in one final attempt to keep me his prisoner unleashed his ultimate weapons of torment. An unexpected panic set in, paralyzing me to my chair and I was suddenly engulfed by its strange power.

An Angelic Vision:

It was as if time stood still; for within seconds, I could see a horde of angelic beings unleashed, positioned, and ready for combat. I could feel the energy that flowed between the two forces. The ones who were named *The Beautiful Ones* were calm but ready for action while the evil and hungry ones were waiting to plunge like famished lions.

The Beautiful Ones carried banners that were made of pure white material and the name *Peace* was written in luminously gold inscriptions. I beheld a glorious white horse, and they called the *Great One* that sat upon it the *Prince of Peace* **(Isaiah 9:6)**. It was a brilliant sight to behold.

When I looked upon the evil ones, I was overtaken by fear that caused my vision of the *Cross* to fade. I saw myself trying to find my way through the obscurity of the night; the light that once was had mysteriously vanished leaving me within the shadows that now surrounded me. As the riders drew nearer and nearer, I clasped my hands over my ears; for the chilling sounds of their hoofs caused earsplitting thundering. I was petrified, scared and all alone.

As the enemy crowded around, they blocked the view of the path making it extremely difficult to find my way. The darkness that lingered along the way was extremely frightening and dreadful and the horses that stood nearby were fearsome; their unsightly countenance was enough to make one run and hide.

I covered my eyes and I could sense they were near because of the stench of rottenness that lingered in the air. I could smell murder, hate, envy and many of the abominable things that the Scriptures spoke about. I had been guilty of some of these things and I began to tremble and weep.

But as I looked toward the hills, I remembered *The Beautiful Ones* I had seen, and I wondered what happened to the strong angelic warriors and the *Great One* whose name was *Prince of Peace*. I knew it was only His mercy that could save me now. But where was He? Why had they not protected me?

Eventually, the vision faded, and I found myself back in the little small church. Though I could not make sense of what was really taking place, I knew that if I did not take this opportunity, it would somehow be my last. But just as I thought it, the pastor proclaimed, *"This may be your last opportunity; for tomorrow is not promised to you. This is your last call."* Then he counted to three. That was all I needed to hear and forgetting the raising of my hand, I flew down the isle before he could call the last number. Sometimes I think I was scared into the Kingdom of Heaven; for the evil mass of demons and the thought of spending eternity separated from God was unbearable.

But it wasn't fear that drew me to the *Cross,* it was His love. The Scripture states that it is God's love that draws and leads us to repentance **(Romans 2:4).** It was His whispers of love that drew me to the *Cross* and His precious *Holy Spirit* at work in my life; pulling and tugging at my heart. He let me know that He would never desert me like others had and that if I opened my heart to Him, He would change my life forever.

As I stood at the altar, I saw the beautiful *Cross* again, and behold, the *One* they called the *Prince of Peace* stood by. As I repeated the sinner's prayer, *The Beautiful Ones* encircled me. Hell's fury was no match against *The Beautiful Ones*. They were unable to withstand the brightness that emanated from their garments causing the evil ones to retreat.

I found myself before this glorious *Cross*, and as I stood before it, I wept like a baby. The *Great One* that had sat upon His horse was now walking toward me. As He approached and knelt down beside me, He placed His loving arms around me; I could feel the power of His forgiveness. He could hear my thoughts and feel my pain as I told Him all that was on my heart and how much I needed Him. I needed Him to show me the road to eternal life because I knew that I could not do it on my own.

We were surrounded by a glorious cloud and all was silent. I told Him that I was afraid of the evil riders and with one wave of His hand they dissipated into thin air. All I could see was just He and me. His touch was warm and I could feel the power of His love flow right through His fingertips. He asked me if He could come into my heart and I answered yes. Suddenly, the silence was broken and a loud uproar rang in celebration **(Luke 15:7)**. He then placed a ring on my finger. I felt as if I was in a marriage ceremony and I was the bride. He said, *"Today you belong to me. I make a covenant with you and that is, to love you and care for you all the* *days of your life. This day, I crown you with the crown of life.",* and with that a magnificent crown was placed on my head. Then someone handed him a beautiful robe and He placed it over my shoulders.

I was immediately dressed in an awesome and amazing armor. I looked like a princess warrior. Not even Xena (a movie character) was arrayed in what I had on. I took a look at my feet and on them was the hottest pair of stilettos I had ever owned. Small pieces of metal were attached on the soles of the shoes to improve my grip during slippery conditions and sets of sharp blades were connected on the upper parts to provide aid for climbing.

A magnificent warrior belt swaddled around my waist; I was warned to never take it off. Within the belt were slots and pouches that automatically opened and closed like an eye. There was also a place for the attachment of my shield and sword.

I could feel the weight of my breastplate and on it were the twelve stones that represented the *Twelve Tribes of Israel* **(Genesis 48:28, Revelation 2:12)**. I somehow knew I belonged to the *Tribe of Judah* **(Genesis 49:10**), but I did not ask how or why. He then instructed me to blow the trumpet in Zion and to sound the alarm **(Joel 2:1**).

He placed a staff in my hands and a book in the other, pointed His finger down a path, and told me to take the road. It was a dark and dismal looking path and I knew that the evil ones were lurking and waiting behind the scenes. I told Jesus that it was impossible for me to see my way because of the gloomy mist. He told me that whenever it got dark and whenever I couldn't find my way, the *Word* which was contained in the *Book* He had given me would illuminate my path. I was warned to guard it with my life.

I was led to a road and by looking at it, I knew that it was not going to be a smooth journey, but with *Jesus* looking on and the *Cloud of Witnesses* on the sidelines, I knew that I would be okay. As I began my journey, I noticed that *Jesus* and the *Cloud of Witnesses* stayed behind. I quickly turned around and asked if they were not coming with me. He answered that He would always be with me **(Matthew 28:20)**.

I opened my eyes and noticed that people from all over the church had approached the altar to hug and welcome me into their church family. I was so happy and I knew that I had begun a new chapter in my life.

Chapter 7

My Mordecai

This little predominant Jamaican church immediately accepted me and I in turn, embraced it with all I had, for I had never come across this kind of attention and love. For the first time in my life, I felt a sense of belonging; I was important and what I had to offer was as equally true. I learned that I was fearfully and wonderfully made and that God loved me **(Psalms 139:14)**. Yes, He loves me; it was evident through the love He expressed on the Cross and by the love I was receiving from His people.

As I adopted the Jamaican culture, my life quickly began to change. I was loved and accepted without feeling threatened in any way. I became one with the people, and I knew this was a place where I could plant my roots, forget about my past, and I knew I would be safe.

My pastor walked very closely to me during the first years of my Christian life. My relationship with him was a wonderful experience. I was embraced by his loving and nurturing ways as he took me under his wings and mentored me. He loved me as his own daughter; just as a shepherd would his sheep. The tender love he offered meant everything to me because I had longed to belong to someone.

I learned many of my life skills under his leadership. He was unbelievably patient, kind and disciplined; something I lacked very much. He modeled forgiveness and expressed how important it was to exhibit it to others when they hurt me. This class wasn't always an easy lesson and many times I failed it. When you are a teenager as rebellious as I was, you lived by the motto, "an eye for an eye and a tooth for a tooth". Many people mistook his kindness for weakness, but he was far from being a weak man. In fact, I learned how to love people in spite of the mistreatment and ridicule and as a result, repeatedly witnessed the favor of God upon his life. His ability to restrain himself in heated situations blew me away every time because I was a lot like Peter; hot-headed, quick tempered, and ready to wield my sword to do some heavy duty cutting **(Mark 14:47).**

Over the years, I learned the principles of sowing and reaping, and as a result, I was blessed tremendously. I was an eye-witnessed to his generosity, for he was a pastor that gave of whatever he had even when he knew he would get nothing in return. The humility that flowed from his heart was something to be desired. Through his life, I was learning about the character of God.

I gained confidence from his meticulous teachings from the Word of God, and my level of faith and trust began to soar in the God I was just getting to know. The love I received from him came at a very crucial time in my life and I was finally experiencing the love of a father. I finally found the father figure I had been searching for all my life.

Chapter 8

The Chameleon

Although I was gradually becoming one with my newfound Christian family, it was during this time that I suppressed the pains of rejection and abandonment and buried them within the deepest part of my soul. Although my spirit was saved, my soul was locked in turmoil.

Oh, I still had unresolved issues that were very much real; inner hurts from the past that had not magically disappeared. Self-rejection surged into my soul like the seismic waves pounding the coastline. The unconscious part of my mind would often influence my behavior without me realizing it, and the mephitic lies would often strike their cords in honor and commemoration of the shame and contempt I felt deep within. My soul needed liberation.

But it was a new beginning and although I was a baby Christian, no one spiritually discerned the troubles I was undergoing. I was experiencing inner turmoil. The real me had been rejected so many times that my secret fear was, would I be rejected again in this newfound family that I had grown to know and love? I had to find a way to outlive this misfortune once and for all. I concluded that Narda Martinez was not accepted by humanity and never would be. Maybe if I could just hide her then, maybe, I would have a chance for some true happiness.

I had somehow convinced myself that by concealing my identity, I would be accepted, well liked and that there would be a chance of being loved. I needed rest from this notorious monster that was expanding like a boletus fungi, but the thoughts and memories of never knowing why I had been abandoned and discarded like a worthless piece of cloth would haunt me in the years to come. My dreams were engulfed with nightmares but I never spoke about it. Talking about it was like removing an old dirty bandage to expose a painfully ugly wound that by now had grown into a deadly Trojan.

Chapter 9

A New Name

I was only fifteen years old when I fell in love. The young man had been serving in the ministry for almost four years and was the drummer for the church. I could not help but to periodically glance over at him during praise and worship as he passionately played the drums.

When I was introduced to him for the first time, his approach was chaste and simple; a mannerism I had never encountered in a young man. We made an immediate connection and it was from that moment that I sensed we would be connected for a very long time.

I thought he was the most wonderful Christian man in the world. I was attracted to his amiable and kind spirited personality. His irresistible pursuit linked me; causing me to yield to the submission of his amorous love.

I never dreamed that anyone could love me the way he did. He infected me with the love and attention he so unfailingly imparted; making me feel valued, beautiful and needed. I was experiencing something I had only dreamed of. He was my knight in shining armor, and I felt like a beautiful Cinderella.

In July of 1988, we married. This was the happiest day of our lives; I could see the pride in his eyes as we swept across the dance floor to our favorite song. His kisses left me breathless and every time I gazed into his eyes, I knew I belonged to him. It was an awesome feeling to belong. I knew I was safe, protected and that he would never allow anyone to hurt me again. I was now Narda Powell. Oh, how I loved my new last name; it gave me an identity I was proud to bear.

Four months after we married, I became pregnant with our first child. Nothing could be more perfect in my world; my dreams of a happy home were all coming true and in August 1989, I gave birth to our first daughter. I could see the look of pride as my husband walked with what Jamaicans would say his chest held high. Ten months later, I was pregnant again and in 1991, I gave birth to another beautiful daughter. Finally, in 1995, we had our third daughter.

I was proud to be a housewife and mother; it was my highest calling as a woman. The opportunity to nurture my children twenty-four seven was a blessing I regarded more significant than anything else; having the luxuries of two incomes was secondary. I was the richest woman on earth and contented with whatever my husband was able to provide.

In the years that followed, we became a dynamic duo. I joined the church choir and eventually became one of the leaders for the praise and worship team. This became my vocal training ground for many years. We became part of the drama group, and many times I wrote plays and skits for special occasions.

Eventually, I became a youth leader; developing and organizing many activities for the Friday night youth services. As I made myself available, my calling in ministry began to surface. My skills began to develop and increase as I found myself studying and teaching on a weekly basis.

I discovered many aspects of my abilities and I learned that I was not as unintelligent as I had believed. As God began to shine His light on me, I was becoming more and more intrigued with discovering the real me; it was like unearthing a treasure box and I could not wait to see what was inside.

The Word of God was my literal source of inspiration and I believed that I could go as far as I wanted to. I fought through my failures, my times of discouragement, fear and the insecurities that people would sometimes impose on me to make me feel that I was just a little uneducated Brooklyn girl.

But my faith and fighting streak was the propelling force that enabled me to go against the grain of the limitations and standards of man's opinion. I was eager and determined to fulfill my destiny and nothing or no one was going to stop me.

Although I was content with my life, from time to time, I dreamed of making teaching my career. But going back to school was not feasible neither a priority at the time. My main concern was spending quality time with my children and making use of every opportunity to equip them for life by training them in the way of the Lord.

As I prayerfully waited, the Holy Spirit would give me the instructions I needed regarding the children. Education began at home and I knew I was my child's first teacher. I was determined to give them a head start in life so I implemented a program of study I put together with the resources I had gathered.

I enjoyed my motherhood; there was nothing more rewarding than seeing the results that followed. I kept a journal of their daily lessons, and by the age of two, the eldest daughter was reading. By this time, my second baby was trailing right behind her; learning quickly everything I was teaching.

I knew as Christian parents, God was going to hold us accountable for what we allowed in our environment and for the things that we permitted to influence their lives. There was a high mandate placed on my life which required that I do everything exactly the way He was instructing me to. I wanted to be found faithful in my garden and committed to the things God had entrusted to me— my family.

I made many mistakes along the way, but I had one plan and one goal, and that was to teach my children the way of life under the heavy scrutiny, guidance, and supervision that came from the Word of God. I only had one opportunity and I wanted to do it right.

By now, I had learned the Jamaican *"way of life."* I was a faithful and devoted wife, a loving mother, and was known by many to keep a tidy home. But while I was a master of all three, I cannot say that I always kept dinner on the table and on time.

He was the sole provider, and although I was unhappy with his extended hours of work, he always made certain that we had all we needed. If there was anything I needed or wanted, he did everything he could to make it happen.

In the fall of 1996, we were on the brink of purchasing our first home. It was a two family semi-attached private home in a fairly nice residential area and also the home we had currently occupied for the past seven years. We had moved to the second floor in hopes of quickly renting out the first floor apartment.

I had scheduled appointments to meet with the three prospective tenants I had found, when my husband unexpectedly announced that we were not going to rent out the apartment again. I asked what we were going to do with an empty apartment and the three people I had found. He told me to cancel them and I did.

Since he was a drum instructor on the weekends and held classes in our music room, my first thoughts was that he intended on opening a music school. But I had the shock of my life when he revealed that we were going to open a Christian daycare. I knew the long hours had taken a toll on his body but now, I thought my husband had completely lost his mind. I panicked as I began to see baby bottles, dirty diapers and hear the cries of snotty nose and screaming children in my head. I had two children and that was enough to keep me busy for the next sixty years. How could he think that all I wanted to do with my life was sit with children all day long?

I became angry at the thought that he could even suggest such a thing. Even my closet friends knew not to ask or volunteer me as a babysitter; my standards were high. The thought of parents dumping their unruly, disobedient and disruptive children into my home made me mad.

I took one good stare at him that my eyes were dancing like jumping beans. I was so mad that I shouted, *"No, we're not!"* His reply was, *"Yes, we are!"* I retorted again, *"No, we're not!"* In the same manner, the *no we're not* and *yes we are* went on for about a minute until he finally got tired and snapped, *"Then I will do it myself!"* I replied, *"Good!"* and with that last shout I sadly ran upstairs.

We did not talk for another two or three hours. I was heated but hurt more than anything else. He had failed to take the time to discuss the matter and find out how I felt or what I thought; after all it would be me who would look after the children, not him. His poorly and mishandled presentation of the idea left my spirit broken and wounded.

But the vision was God given, and regardless of how it was delivered it did not diminish or deplete its purpose. We must always be aware that the message(s) God gives us to convey to others is not done in confusion, selfishness or pride. We can cause unnecessary hurt, misunderstandings and sometimes damage to others when we mishandle or do not deliver God's Word or instruction properly.

Nonetheless, when we spoke that evening, I knew that he was the one God chose to impregnate me with the vision of opening a Christian daycare. Unlike the first, his second attempt was very successful. His approach came with encouraging words; breaking down the towers of my defenses and allowing him to speak into my life.

He commended me on how well I had been working with our girls and that he also admired the way I directed the youth group. He further reminded me that since I had always wanted to teach, this would open a great opportunity for me to further develop my teaching skills. He encouraged me not to allow the negativity of not having a high school diploma keep me from reaching the goal. He assured me that I had what it took to teach.

As he spoke, it was as if he was breathing life into the dreams that lay dormant. My spirit rose in confidence and my partner was confirming the call of God on my life. He saw beyond the logical and physical limitations and his faith linked with mine began to cause a whirlwind of supernatural blessings to unfold.

It was in early December of 1996 that *Noah's Ark Christian Academy* (formerly named *ABC + 123 Christian Academy*) was birthed. We had a lot of work to do and little time, so we executed a plan of action and went to work as quickly as possible.

My spouse was a striving entrepreneur. He had his own business of renovating homes and had become quite popular within our city. He led the remodeling process while I worked on getting my license and paperwork; obtaining any information I could find for the purpose intended.

I remember the day he first took the sledge hammer to knock out the wall that divided what was once our master bedroom and the girl's room. I was at the doorway watching, and in that split second, the Lord spoke to my heart. You see, God was telling us to cast out nets on the other side of the boat **(Luke 5:4-**

5). In other words, be willing to step out in faith and launch out into the deep. We were crossing waters we had never crossed before, but His response of loving affirmation and promises of provision for the vision gave me a confidence that propelled me like a bullet.

I had no idea where to begin, no knowledge on how to start a business, and no prior experience in business management. There was the added fact that I did not have the information or resources for the things I needed for my preschool. But as promised, God directed me every step of the way.

One snowy and cold night, I was on my way to pick up my daughters who had spent the day with their grandmother. As I drove up to the snowbound area, I was reminded that my daughter's godmother who lived right across the street had asked me to stop by and pick up a Christmas present she had for her. I decided to pay her a quick visit.

It was so cold that night that I could not wait to get into the house where it was nice and warm. It had been a while since I had last seen her, so when we got to talking, I updated her about the girls, family life, etc. When I shared with her my plans to open a preschool and that it was already under construction, she happily rejoiced. She was a teacher herself and had been working in the public school system for several years.

Coincidently, there happened to be a school exposition that was being held in the city for all public school principals, teachers, and directors the following day. She graciously asked if I would be her guest and I enthusiastically accepted. She brought me up to date and informed I would receive information regarding everything I needed to get my business started.

Talk about God-links, I was overjoyed and thrilled at knowing that the Father had once again shone His light on a dim course. I told her that I would not miss it for the world and that I would meet her bright and early in the morning.

As promised, I showed up full of excitement and with great expectation. When we arrived, I was amazed to see the amount of professionals that attended; teachers and principals, and directors of known programs and schools were all there. I was honored to be among these fine people.

It was more than I expected. It reminded me of a student book fair; every educational publication was present and their booths were colorfully arrayed. They held sessions and class demonstrations for teachers to use in correlation with their school curriculum. I took every catalog, brochure, and business card. Even if I did not think I would use it, I took it anyway.

When I got home, I tended to my blistered fingers I received as a result of carrying the many bags I toted around. But I did not mind because all I could think about was looking through the material I had in my possession. The resources to everything I needed to start my preschool were at my fingertips.

Needless to say, over the years, the preschool blossomed. Excellence became our signature and every year we ironed out the kinks and implemented new ideas. I strategically structured my appointments; interviews were a minimum of forty-five minutes to an hour. I wanted the parents of the children that enrolled in our school to be aware of our program's mission and the purpose for our existence. We were not babysitters or some drop-off joint; we were a learning academy with a mission statement, a philosophy and a standard of conduct that was expected for all, parent, student, faculty and staff.

I developed all registration forms, contracts, handbooks and manuals that we would use and every year updated them. I created and personally designed my own business cards and stationeries, yearbooks, flyers, brochures and anything that could be used for marketing purposes. Each of us happily committed ourselves to our work, and during the first three years, both businesses began to soar tremendously.

At the same time, we continued to minister in song for many years. We visited nursing homes, participated in church banquets and choirs, concerts and other church affiliated events. Sometimes I went solo, no live band; just a little music box and tape.

We freely gave; never receiving a tithe or an offering from any person or ministry. One of the first principles we had learned from our spiritual parents was to freely give, freely receive. But I was naive about the logistics of ministry; the planning and implementation of a complex task was something I really knew nothing about. The propelling force of any ministry is in its operation and a poorly managed business will not be successful. It takes money to run a company and it was going to take money to accomplish our ministry goals.

Over the years, key players in the group became discontent and began their gripe about getting paid for gigs. It was difficult finding people who were likeminded; people who would help carry out the mandate and vision that God had given, and the idea of charging money made me uncomfortable and uneasy. But with an understanding of the Scriptures concerning a man being worthy of his hire, it became easier to charge when appropriate.

Many of the musicians we used were independent freelancers who had devoted their life to being fulltime musicians, so we only charged the cost to pay them; never taking anything for ourselves.

But accomplishing God's will did not come without facing ministry hardships. As the appointments began to increase, so did the financial demands. I discovered that no longer were people willing to minister unless there was some compensation. Ministries never gave love offerings to help pay for our expenditures, so we took care of them from our personal finances.

There were times I did become discouraged and often times rejected appointments. To add to this, the discontent and frustration we were experiencing over the years in our church were enlarging and was a direct result of inadequate and ineffective managerial skills. That is, the inability for a collaborate workforce to be set in place. But no ministry is birthed in perfection and what ministry did not have their idiosyncratic faults.

But I still had my idealistic views about leadership; most of us do. My biggest mistake was to ever place high expectations on my leaders. It would seem almost impossible to expect busy pastors especially with large congregations to walk with me the way I had imagined. My outlook of what I thought leaders should be were excessive and unrealistic; too many sheep, too many issues. Then the problem of having over anxious inexperienced leaders eagerly waiting to take on matters they were unequipped for troubled me. I concluded that I was still a novice and resolved that my leaders were likewise struggling and by faith walking out what God had called them to do.

But just as with any relationship, if there is no honest communication, things can go awry. Shepherds and sheep sometimes don't always see eye to eye. Overwhelmed pastors lose sight of the little but significant things that his people undergo, and by the same token, we also fail to see the extent and sacrifice our pastors make. My pastors were good shepherds, and they gave their best. While trying to raise an army of leaders, there was no way that they could give any more than they already had; their season in our lives had been fulfilled and it was now time to move on.

There are some great things that can be learned if we choose to remain where the Lord wants us to be; for it is in the midst of ministry inadequacies and personal imperfections that the Lord uses the very things that have worked against us as mere tools to sharpen us. God uses **ALL THINGS** whether good or bad for the sole purpose of bringing us into our destiny.

In retrospect, the failures we experience within the course of ministry are designed to prepare us for tomorrow. The billows that roll in the darkness of night should cause us to seek Him with our whole hearts. We can allow the negative events we experience to cripple our future or we can choose to learn from them.

In spite of setbacks, God will always provide landmarks and signs to help us get to our destination. He gives us landmarks of wrong and right directions; dead-end and wrong turn symbols, detours, yield and stop signs that tell us where we are, where we have been and where we are going. Instead of blaming the Lord for the layout or pattern of the journey, we should take responsibility for the decisions we make and resist the opportunity for blaming the pastors, the church or God for where we are.

The phases or periods of experiencing revolutionary breakthroughs, low points, or rock bottom moments are inevitable. Every sailor knows that someday he will face turbulent weather. It is his responsibility to train and exercise caution and to know the warning signs. Likewise, the designated driver is also responsible for knowing and reviewing the course of his journey. He is under heavy obligation to be aware of the signs of the road; failure to recognize or obey the signs of the road could lead to fatal or regrettable consequences.

Similarly, when we accept Jesus Christ into our hearts, we are very much like that designated driver or sailor. We are given the keys to life and a roadmap which is the *Bible*. During the course, we learn to recognize the various signs of the road, explore unfamiliar territory, and are subjected to hazardous conditions, unpredictable weather and the various changes of the speed limit.

Paul admonishes us to run the race with patience **(Hebrews 12:1)**. Failure to comply with the rules of our spiritual journey will often time take us off course, leading us to the physical and spiritual dead-ends or somewhere in a back alley. It is our impatience, disobedience, ignorance and self-will that hinder us from attaining our goal.

There are various factors as to why one loses his way in life; a simple missing or making of a wrong turn, a failure to read the road signs, following the wrong directions or having insufficient information regarding the destination could all lead to one thing—not arriving at the expected end or at the appointed time.

Chapter 10

The Gate

The *Cross* is where life began for me. The *Cross* is the gate or the door that leads to everlasting life. It is the place where those who say yes to Jesus experience a transformed life; a place of relinquishing and handing over the broken pieces of your life to a loving and kind Savior. It is the place of a *Divine Exchange*; your old, troubled and wounded life for an amazing inner peace and life everlasting from the *One* who is the *Prince of Peace*. Old things are past away and all things become new **(II Corinthians 5:17)**.

However, this new life does not mean that you will not be subjected to trials and temptations or experience victories and defeats. You will still undergo some sad days, mad days and days when you may feel like pulling your hair out (if you have any) or maybe someone else's.

It does not mean that the problems you encountered yesterday, today, or tomorrow will magically vanish away by saying some fairytale chant of abracadabra. It just simply means that if you know Him, you'll trust Him to give you the wisdom, knowledge and the strength to make it through every situation.

But learning is a process; it is a life-long daily walk with the Savior. When you spend quality time with someone, you get to know all about them. You see, God is about relationship; something most of us know really nothing about. Even when we come to know Christ, we still don't know everything. We are like babes who are forever learning and forever growing.

Our parents and guardians were our first teachers. While some of us may have had good parents, many had none, or worse, had really bad ones. We only know what was taught and model before us on a daily basis and whether positive or negative, we must admit it has had a great impact on our ability or inability to function in this life. For this reason, when we become born-again, God has to tear down our old way of thinking because some of our philosophies and ideologies are corrupt and twisted. We must be willing to learn all over again and sometimes that can prove to be very difficult.

In the born-again experience, it is the spirit man or the inner man that gets saved **(Ephesians 4:22).** However, your flesh (the physical part of you) remains the same; your looks and body structure doesn't change, although for some of us it would be a great improvement. Your voice, hair and the color of eyes do not change either. But what does begin to change is the way you think; and it all starts with an inner change of the heart.

A new desire is birthed within you; a genuine longing for God springs forth in you. And because you love the Lord, it also means that your old way of thinking becomes submissive to the new order of God's way; even if it conflicts with your right to be right. It is a putting away of the old man (the flesh), with its: "*I want to do it my own way attitude*" **(Colossians 3:9)**.

But you will find that your flesh has a big mouth. It is the greatest dictator you will ever come to know. Unfortunately, it is a part of you; a part you will take everywhere you go until you die. For many years, your flesh has been governed by its sinful nature. It has followed its own desires and laws, hates authority, and does not like to be told what to do. It seeks to live without restrictions or limits; in simple terms, it prefers its own way. It is your personality and the passionate part of you that takes action in a negative or positive way. This is why we must be led by the Spirit of God to avoid fulfilling the lust of the flesh **(Romans 8:14)**.

As a child of God, your flesh will go undergo vigorous rehabilitation. The more you learn about God's Word the more your life will gradually change. The Word of God has the power to transform you more and more into His image **(Romans 8:29)**. You will find that the sins you once took pleasure in no longer appeal to you. Your new aspiration to lead a righteous life now commands your flesh to catch up with your spirit.

Christianity is not a religion but a way of life. It is a disciplined life that will sometimes take every muscle, every tissue, and every cell in your being to make the right choice. It is saying in times of confusion and adversity, I will seek and trust God's counsel and not my own **(Proverbs 3:5)**. The comfort I receive when faced with challenges is that the Lord is with me, and if I don't succeed the first time, I can always try again.

I know first hand what it feels like to face mountains that seem impassable, but over the years, I have learned to go through with God one time then repeating the lesson again and again. Believe me when I tell you that a lesson repeated is a lesson not learned. The children of Israel repeated a lesson for forty years **(Joshua 5:6)**. I don't have forty years, heck, I don't have two years to waste. I read the historical accounts of the children of Israel, and they serve as a reminder that when we disobey, murmur and complain, or choose to do things on our own, we just spin around our wheels never getting anywhere.

Everyone has issues or mountains they must hurdle. Never think for one minute that you are alone or the only one. Millions of people were facing the same mountain all at the same time. There will always be something in your life that you are trying to work out. Whether it is insecurity, or an addiction to drugs, sex or pornography, anger, stealing, you like to tell exaggerated stories, dishonesty, or you find that you are a very jealous person, or something else you may feel you cannot share with anyone, the list goes on. But, be it the latter or the first, you face issues everyday of your life and sometimes they can wear you down.

Then there are the deeper psychological and emotional wounds like you may hate yourself, you may feel rejected or unloved. You may even have thoughts of suicide or you may have been raped or molested as a child and haven't told anyone. You may have had an abortion twenty or thirty years ago and still struggle with the guilt.

These mountains in your life may seem undefeatable. It may look like an impossible or impassable situation and you may feel like your life will never change. Please understand that God will not always remove a mountain. Sometimes He wants you to face them; for there are many lessons to learn in the valleys of your life that you will never experience anywhere else. Be strong, don't quit, stay the course, and remember, whatever your lot, God always knows what He's doing, even if you don't.

When you are faced with the challenges of life, if you yield your heart towards God, He will strengthen you and help you. God wants to heal you and bring you to a place of complete wholeness.

Healing involves a process of bringing or restoring wholeness and sound functioning to every aspect of the human life. The English word *health* literally means "wholeness," and so *to heal* means "to make whole." It includes the body (physical), soul (emotional and mental stability), and spiritual aliveness (spirit). This broad-based definition sometimes includes what is popularly known as "inner healing," where the focus is more specifically on psychological and emotional wounds and their repair **(Encarta ® World English Dictionary).**

For years my flesh had been enslaved to sin **(Romans 6:14),** but my new birth in Christ was the beginning to a new order; a new government and a new way of thinking that conflicted with the old.

In this new life, I am commissioned to become conformed into God's image **(Romans 8:29).** The word *conform* does not mean to *change*; *conform* is the act or molding process that brings about the result of change. *Conform* is a verb (*action word*) and *change* is a noun (*a state of being*); you cannot become changed without first applying the act to change.

There is a responsibility placed on the believer for personal growth. Conformation is not automatic as some may suppose; it is a bringing of one thing into accord with another, and in this case, it is a yielding or surrendering of our will to God.

Your flesh will always undergo constant pressure for godly conformation. This new life or governing body that had now streamlined into my spirit and heart was classified as an intruder by my flesh. The flesh will have fits; throw fights, resist, argue, scream, dictate, hurl tantrums and even hold pity parties in full rebellion to the fixed standard, regulations and requirement of God's laws. It revolts in uprising mutiny because from its inception, it has known no other way. This is why we have got to behave acceptably, follow the standard and obey the rules of God's order so that transformation can eventually take place.

The *Cross* is the *door* or the *gate* by which you first enter to receive forgiveness of sins and the promise of eternal life. You do not receive the benefits that come with the finished work of the *Cross* until you first enter and become an heir. Once you've entered, you are a legal son or daughter and the prime beneficiary holder of God's promises.

But never think for one minute that because you are a Christian that you are not capable of sinning in what Christendom would consider "*in the worst way*". Sin is sin as far as God is concerned. Many of God's people are lifelessly paddling in the waves of their mistakes; never forgiving themselves because they never thought they could commit such crimes against God or others. There are many Biblical examples of great men falling but just as many finding redemption, healing and restoration through a forgiving and loving Savior.

God does not hover over us with a bat to strike us every time we fail. He understands that some of life's lessons can be very difficult and that it can take more than one try to get it right. God understands our past hurts and is very patient, loving and merciful toward us **(Psalms 103:8)**. He is our personal cheerleader; always nearby to cheer us on.

But our faith in God is only stretched and strengthened when it is put under extreme pressure. Weight lifters gain the strength in their muscles from their consistent practice of weight training, so let the trials of your life toughen your muscles of faith so that you can soar like eagles **(Isaiah 40:31)**.

Chapter 11

The Game

But who was I really? I had been the daughter of a docile mother and a ruthless father before knowing Jesus Christ. I learned only what I lived and lived what I had learned; a product of my environment.

The *Cross* was the door and the beginning of my journey. The *Cross* provided not only forgiveness and salvation, but an immense of unlimited blessings and promises such as healing, prosperity, victory over my trials and a joy that is unspeakable and full of glory to name a few.

But I did not get it all at one time, and before further healing and deliverance from the ancestral curses that plagued my family could take place, as an enlisted soldier in the Lord's Army, I had much to learn. I had to know my rival, the players, and how they strategically functioned as a team.

It was crucial that I understood my purpose in life – the reason I was created. But this would all begin with understanding my position as a child of God. A true knowledge of who I was would wreak much destruction on the enemy's kingdom. This is why he tries to keep us blind to the revelation of God's Word. He knows that when we know the truth it means trouble for him.

With the guidance of the Holy Spirit, I would be able to identify and detect the root of any problems that surfaced in my personal life; like the governing roots and principalities that caused me to feel inferior or less than anything God said I was.

Understanding my opponent, how he functioned and the tactics he used would appear a bit complicated because the deceitful and scheming chameleon comes in various forms. But I was determined to understand him, and the only way to accomplish this was knowing what the Bible had to say about him.

The Bible classifies him as the accuser of the brethren and the father of lies **(John 8:44)**. He will use the inners hurts and memories of your past to keep you from achieving your purpose in life. But how does he accomplish this? You must remember that he has been here since the time of creation. He has records of your past that dates back to your first ancestors in the Garden of Eden. He knows more than you think and he is shrewd and very skilled in how to play his game.

I read in a *Dear Abby* article recently about a mother who had great concerns about her little boy who was only six. She was so terrified about her son's future that her fears kept her up at night. The boy's father had a history of drugs and alcohol abuse and she was afraid that genetically her son was predisposed to the addiction. She wanted to know if there was an established, proven course of action that she could take to prevent future horrors.

While *Dear Abby's* response was sound and practical, the fears the mother possessed bothered me. FEAR is *false evidence appearing real*. The enemy was using fear and the father's drug and alcohol history to dictate the negative likelihood of her son's future. Even though it had not yet happened, her fears opened the door to insomnia and the anxieties she probably quite often experiences. She somehow believes that as the father is, so will the son be.

Does this sound familiar? It should because the Bible tells us that we are predestined to become the children of God **(Ephesians 1:5)**. It is not in the Father's plan that any should perish but that all receive everlasting life through His son Jesus Christ **(John 3:15)**. However, we are not forced, just as this son in the future will not be forced to use drugs although genetically predisposed to it. If he is led to believe that he is like his father, then he will become just like his father; for as a man thinks in his heart, so is he **(Proverbs 23:7)**.

Just as we were genetically through the fall of Adam predisposed to death because of sin, God has given each of us the power of choice to change the outcome of a hopeless future. He said there is life and death before you, and then He tells us which to choose **(Deuteronomy 30:19)**.

The enemy uses all kinds of tools to inflict damage in the lives of people. The younger you are the better; molestation and rape, betrayal, rejection and abandonment from loved ones, violence and drugs are all gateways for the enemy to slither through to inflict the wounds that seem to forever haunt us. Most hurts remain suppressed and lodged in the compartments of our hearts; never to be spoken about again.

It is for this very reason that the Lord desires to put a final end to the miserable disease that has infected our souls. But a refusal to talk about it or face it will only delay God's healing in the life of the individual, and a result, it can keep you from becoming whole.

Once I entered through the *Gate*, it would be a very long and narrow road. My experiences were only calculated trainings with intended goals to give me a broader and clearer prospective on the realities I would face as a devout Christian. My encounter as a former POW (the devil's former **prisoner** *of war*) served to better equip me for the many combats ahead. **Jeremiah 29:11** says, **"*I know the plans I have for you...to give you an expected.*"**

Chapter 12

Spirit and Truth

Little did I know that in the years to come, my life as I knew it and everything I held dear to my heart would be shattered one after the other. In 1999, my husband and I were ordained as music ministers and received the blessings from our spiritual parents. During this time, my unquenchable thirst and longing for God led me to a desperate pursuit of His presence.

There had to be more to Christianity than fulfilling my weekly church routine. No longer did the formality of being in the choir, drama group or music satisfy me. No one understood what I was undergoing and many thought I was neglecting my church duties. Some labeled it backsliding and you could hear the whispers and the targeted messages that occasionally flowed from the pulpit. But backsliding was far from being my dilemma.

God Himself had permitted the reformation and streamlining that was taking place. The emptiness, purposeless and unfulfilling disposition that had now overwhelmed me made absolutely no sense. I loved the Lord and I wanted more than anything to serve Him. But why was I feeling so unsatisfied and empty in doing what I had been doing for so long? I felt stifled; somehow as if I had been placed in a box that no longer fit and I wanted out whatever the cost.

But I would never have imagined the price I'd pay to answer the Master's call. We knew our season in our local church was over. Many thought we had left due to the problems the ministry was encountering and while some things may have been a contributing factor, the Lord was shaking our nest.

How do you logically explain to people that the Lord is calling you out of a ministry that you have grown up in all your life without being harshly judged? **You don't!** I am certain Abraham and Sarah must have felt the same way when God called them to leave their extended families, the comfort of their home and everything they ever knew and move to an unfamiliar place they had never heard of, been to or seen. How crazy did that sound?

To be honest, I was glad to be free from all church obligations and the responsibilities that I was tied to. It had nothing to do with the people because I loved them so dearly but a disappointment that the people we had faithfully served for so long did not recognize the calling of God on our lives. But God knew. . .

It was as if there were similarities with my father and my spiritual daddy. Although my father never wanted anyone of us to leave home, it isn't logically realistic or healthy to think or believe that the children you raise will never leave home one day.

Because of insecurity and control issues, my father never learned how to release his children so that they could become good and productive citizens. Even within the church walls, I found a similar problem existing.

Shepherds are like fathers, and their role is very much equivalent to that of a parent. A shepherd seeks to guide and protect his flock, while at the same time making sure that they are properly provided for and fed. The health and strength of his herd depends on his ability to manage, lead and guide.

But on the other hand, there is a misconception that pastors and churches are perfect entities. I have had the privilege of walking beside many great men and women of God and my experiences with them have caused me to repent many times and not judge prematurely a person, issue or case before sufficient evidence is available. But my inclinations to high expectations often led to much disappointment.

Please allow me to share with you what I discovered pastors are not. Pastors are not supermen and women but human beings with feelings like you and me. They are not a twenty-four seven eleven spiritual pharmaceutical or super-chronic crisis center where you can conveniently drive through their lives and check out any time you feel like it.

Most times they rather be playing ball with the guys or out shopping with the ladies. They like to read books, watch movies and swim. They are normal people who like to do normal things. They get teed off and don't like having their intimate moments interrupted by the telephone to deal with something that could have waited for the next day. They make mistakes, get discouraged and are often pulled in every direction from thoughtless folks who don't receive the counsel given or who fail to follow instructions. Yet, these are the same folks that expect you to be there for them and then have the nerve to get mad if you're not.

They have stories of triumphs and defeat and everyday face challenges in their relationships, business and family life. They don't have perfect children as some suppose and suffer the same hurt and embarrassment you do when your child does something wrong. To add to this, they are ridiculed, talked about, lied on and simply the topic of many hardhearted after service conversations.

While the expectations of pastors are high and in some cases unrealistic, they somehow pull through the harsh conditions and amazingly and faithfully continue to fulfill their church responsibilities week after week.

Some pastors are gentle and kind while others are rough and insensitive. You have good pastors who really care about their people and then there are others who really care nothing at all. Some are governed and led by the Spirit of God while others are led by the powerless traditions of their ancestors that date back to the 18th century. Some are passive, yet others are aggressive. Then you have the controlling and arrogant pastors who use guilt as a form of power.

Over the years, I witnessed shepherds fighting over sheep as if they were some type of furniture that looked better in their corner. Ministers refusing to network with others due to the lack of confidence that stemmed from within their own hearts or lack of training. Pastors who made you feel guilty because you chose to visit another ministry or simply decided to spend that long overdue time with your family on that Sunday morning.

I have witnessed pastors spiritually abuse God's people; publicly insulting and humiliating them to a point where they physically walked out of church. I've seen many carelessly use the pulpit as their source of weapon; not realizing that their behavior was indirectly teaching others to do the same. I have seen it all and I was sick of it.

Wounded pastors were feeding God's sheep and because hurting people hurt other people, the pattern continued. They themselves have not dealt with the scars of their wounded past and so the spiritual fathers that we grow to love and respect disappointingly hurt us.

This is why many of the spiritual children that shepherds give birth to run away. As children, we vow never to make the same mistakes our parents or spiritual parents made, only to find that the fruit never really falls far from its tree.

After we left, we went an entire year without attending any local church. An occasional visit to any church was more than enough for me and since I had been greatly wounded in ministry, I vowed that *"church membership"* would never again be in my vocabulary. We had been sheltered for as long as God allowed and now about to embark on a journey of faith.

But neither of us had any indication about the many giants that were dwelling in the land; awaiting our dare to cross over. But in case Goliath and his brothers decided they wanted a fight, I was ready to give them one. I made sure to pick up my five smooth stones.

Here we faced the biggest storms of our lives; for many undulant trials and hardships were looming. But even in the midst of much uncertainty and though trouble was on every side, I somehow knew that God would be with us.

I continued to daily listen and watch the **Joyce Meyers and Creflo Dollar's online broadcast.** While I made it a consistent practice to stay in the Word, my husband's carelessness and neglect of his spiritual and marital responsibilities increased. He continued to work, coming home late every evening; never making the time to sit with us for any type of family time or devotion.

I made plans to visit churches only, sit, watch and leave like everyone else; making no real commitment to the work of the Lord. But deep within, I knew that my life no longer belonged to me and that I would soon have to answer His call. Eventually, my plans were interrupted by the sovereign plan of the Most High.

Over the years, I have discovered that it is in the disorder of life, broken hearts and shattered dreams that God begins to construct His most beautiful masterpiece. God's divine plan was unfolding in the midst of turmoil and upheaval. Yes, God was birthing greatness.

In January of 2000, we ministered in a small Mount Vernon church not far from where we lived. The ministry was relatively young with about six to seven years of operation and was growing rapidly. Each department within the ministry was made up of industrious believers who seemed rather sincere in their work for the Lord. I had never seen a bunch of committed Christians like *Family Christian Center.*

As time went by, the ministry became in need of a drummer because their former drummer was relocating; it seemed too perfect. A drumming position is usually never available and it is exclusive to members only. There is usually a waiting list that is full of eager young men anxious to be next in line but the door was opened for my husband; a non-member!

I visited occasionally with no real intention of ever becoming a member or giving of myself and the gifts that God had equipped me with. As I stated earlier, my plans were to sit, warm the pew and leave service with no real commitment.

But as I began visiting more often, major reconstruction began to take place in my heart. God began to unearth the roots to the colossal towers that held my soul a prisoner. The lethal corrosion that flooded my life through these illegal tunnels and venues had been stained with treacherous lies that had caused severe damage to my self-esteem.

These conduits had specialized agents whose job was to blur my vision and keep me from ever seeing myself as God had seen me. But on the other hand, every time the Word went forth, it surgically amputated the filthy residues of shame and rejection that had engrossed itself against my soul over the years. Only the expertise of my Father's Sword would now bring the dividing of my wounded soul and spirit.

I recognized that my new pastors were not perfect but gifted with much wisdom, and more importantly, that they were the ones God had assigned for the next phase of my life. I must admit that this pair of shepherds was an intriguing couple; I had never before met any duo like them. They had experienced much in life and what made them most effective was the simple and practical way they ministered. They were not afraid to share their personal successes as well as personal failures and defeats. Week after week, they continually poured into my spirit truth that flowed from the heart of God, bringing the deliverance I so desperately needed. I fed on the truths they imparted and the genuine interest they demonstrated in my life ignited the possibility of trusting again.

As I quietly sat during each service, God began to speak in earth-shattering volumes. I had never heard nor felt the presence of God so strongly in my life. My heart quaked with the pounding sounds of each word spoken. Sometimes I cried through entire services, each time being left broken before God. I was named the weeping prophet by the very few that I had allowed into my world.

I had no clue that *Family Christian Center*, formerly named *Spirit & Truth International Ministries* would become our new home. I walked circumspectly, careful not to become attached to any particular person, group or department. I isolated myself for almost two years, while my husband happily committed himself to the music department. The thought of becoming connected made me nervous; for I had given so much before only to be disappointed and hurt. This was one experience I did not want to repeat.

I carefully watched to observe how the people and church affairs were handled, and while I was not looking for perfect pastors or a perfect church, I was looking for leaders who were committed to help bring the purpose and call of God in my life into fruition. I did not want '*empire builders*', or ministries who were looking to build pretty churches, but shepherds who had God's heart for the sheep and for the building of His kingdom. I wanted the pastors that **Jeremiah 3:15** spoke about: **"And I will give you pastors according to mine heart, which shall feed you with knowledge and understanding."**

But it was not until I trusted my pastors that I was able to begin dealing with the real issues in my life. It was around the dinner table one evening when my pastor first dove into my personal life. His perceptive and insightful assessment of the pride I once experienced when several Latin women were named as runners up for the Miss USA contest was the beginning of a revolutionary war in my soul. I needed to know why I experienced a moment of self-worth, only for it to be almost instantly devalued and diminished by my own embittered internal response. It made no sense.

I thought God demonstrated his good sense of humor when He gave me a pastor that was half-Latin and half-Jamaican. The hand of God orchestrated even this very important detail, for he understood my background as a Latina, as well as, my Jamaican cultural upbringing. He had gone through a similar identity issue and seemed to be the only person that really understood me; sometimes more than I understood myself. He related to my emotional hullabaloo and I began to slowly trust him. I had finally connected with someone who genuinely understood me; someone who would help me put things in perspective. I was in dire search for the real me so who else to talk with than one who had been down that road.

But the sincere and genuine spirit my pastors moved in was not enough to cry out for immediate help, for again, my fears, lack of trust and pride would time and time hinder me from unlocking the pain I bottled up over the years.

Many times I visited the church office, calling it my little getaway. But it was more in hopes that one day I would find my way onto the office couch for a one to one session. Pastor would often ask, *"What's up, Nahnah?"* Boy did I want to divulge all. I wanted to finally let the cat out of the bag but I was too afraid; for my cat was a big puss.

I knew that he knew I needed to talk but he never imposed; he just patiently waited. I was very apprehensive for a long time. The fear of being rejected and to face the possibility of betrayal was something I dreaded the most. How could I share my most personal and intimate life with them? What would they think of me or worse, how would they react afterward? I decided to play it safe and wait.

As I entered my second year at *Family Christian Center*, I continued to observe carefully the lives of the people in leadership. Since I had deep-rooted issues with trust, talk was cheap and what people said no longer impressed me.

I was in search for real leadership, real Christians, real pastors; someone who would be transparent. Again, I was not looking for perfect pastors or a perfect church but I was looking for honest and genuine people who shared the same common denominator **"brokenness"**.

It was during personal fellowship, women's meetings, and retreats that I had the opportunity to listen to the testimonies of the people I had begun to admire and respect. Experiences had ranged from personal classified issues to municipal litigations. Sometimes God's people behave so badly it can turn you off.

I attentively listened as my pastors and others shared their personal and intimate stories; some were success stories and some were complete failures, but they seemed to cover all topics of life. I was experiencing Real Life 101, and these saints of God were for real.

I was encouraged and ministered to each time personal testimonies were shared. Some were truly transparent and it was powerful enough to make me see that I was not in this battle alone. Many of them had encountered brutal assaults from the enemy just as I had. Some stories were worse than my own and yet they had amazingly overcome. God was lucratively using these people and their testimony to bring deliverance into my life.

My thought process was gradually changing as I saw truth and humility flow from the lives of His people. They had been well discipled and their lifestyle was living proof.

The Truth about My Marriage:
In the year 2000, my husband applied for his US citizenship but without my knowledge had been denied. The cause for denial was kept a secret. I remember the morning he left to take the exam. He appeared jittery, so I said a prayer for him and told him to stay encouraged.

When he returned that afternoon, as usual, I greeted him at the door, threw my arms around him and congratulated him. He had studied so hard, and I was more than confident that he had passed. I asked a few questions about the meeting, and then we went about the rest of the day like any other day.

But the truth of that day would not be revealed until two years later. He had been denied his United States citizenship due to bigammy. His marriage to another woman many years earlier had not been properly annulled, therefore, making our marriage of fourteen years of none effect and no-existence. In the two years that followed and in efforts of sparing me any hurt, he kept it quiet, while he secretly sought lawyers; each one advising him that he needed to tell me.

In the summer of 2002, he finally told me the truth of that day. I worried as we sat in our vehicle. We parked on Bronx Boulevard for almost half an hour before he could utter a full sentence. As I patiently waited for him to release what was on his heart, I observed that he was having an extremely difficult time. While he was nervous and edgy, my heart was filled with anxiety and fear. I had no idea what he was about to disclose.

As he fumbled and stuttered around with his words, I interrupted to question if it was another woman or if he had a baby that I did not know about; but both were a no and I was relieved. I then proceeded to asked if he was gay, since I could not imagine anything else but the long gawp his face delivered immediately alerted me about my brainless and witless line of questioning.

There was a long and dead silence as I wondered what in the world could the man that I adored and thought the world of tell me that was so horrible. Creflo Dollar's teaching tape that was playing in the background broke the silence when he said that honesty had to be the first step in order for a marriage to begin the healing process. Call it perfect timing but the encouraging words he heard gave him the boost he needed.

I could feel my face turning pale as he revealed that we were not legally married. It was the beginning of a horrible nightmare; I could not believe what I was hearing. If I was not Narda Powell, then who the heck was I? Surely not Narda Martinez; I had done away with her a long time ago and there was no way I could still be her! I felt sick.

But I told him that I loved him and that I would never leave him because of it; I thought his fear of losing me over it was the reason he had hidden it for so long. We then briefly talked about the steps we needed to take to fix the problem, after which he stepped out of the car and said he wanted to walk home alone. I did not want him to leave; how could he walk away and leave me alone at a moment like this? But I gave him the space he needed to clear his head.

I no longer wanted to pretend that everything was great in my world. I wanted to finally tell someone the truth that I was not as wonderful and strong as many thought. I sped my way onto the highway and headed for the church office. Maybe my pastors could point me in the right direction or the least give me some moral support; God knows I needed some.

When I got there, I headed straight into Pastor Sherri's office. By the time I entered, I was shaking and I could tell she sensed my urgency as she got up to close the door. The news caught her off guard as her big beautiful eyes grew twice the size. She did not say anything but walked toward me and place her arms around me.

I cried and cried and she held me in her arms. Then she whispered, *"It's going to be okay; the same thing happened to me and you're going to be okay."* I thought my ears were playing tricks on me, and with that thought she took one look at me and said she would be right back. As she walked out to get Pastor Mott, I wondered was there anything this couple had not been through.

When she walked back in, you could see an overwhelming expression on Pastor Mott's face. He took a seat and I began to tell them both the whole story. But Pastor Sheri's account of what happened to her made it a lot easier for me to deal with what seemed to be the most devastating news of my life.

By the time I left their office, I was feeling a lot better than when I had first walked in. It wasn't as bad as it sounded; it was only a matter of paperwork and that could be fixed. I made an appointment to meet with them again, this time with my husband.

Chapter 13

The Battle

It was in January of 2003, when I first discovered my husband's infidelity. I was searching for tax papers in a box where we kept most of our business documents when I came across a little wrinkled note.

My heart bled tears as I read the note in my quivering hands over and over. It felt like a knife was repeatedly plunging into it slashing and tearing at it without mercy. I had never been subjected to such pain like I experienced that day. The man I thought the world of would never be capable of such disloyalty. But there it was in his own writing; the evidence that he clearly had been unfaithful and broken the covenant that I held so sacred.

For a long time, I felt nothing but numbness. What was I going to do? How would I handle the situation? Was this the end of our marriage, our family and could I survive the terror that was about to unfold?

I was scared as I confronted him that evening. He was very nervous as he responded that he was sorry and that it was water under the bridge for him; something that he wanted to forget ever happened.

My entire night was filled with tears. For a total of nineteen years, I had faithfully loved him. As I rested on the daycare mats that had become our bed, I wondered where we went wrong. He was all I had known since the age of fifteen and my best friend.

I knew our relationship wasn't perfect; we had arguments like any other couple but I was happy and had resolved that I'd love him forever. I had placed so much confidence and trust in him that I never believed that he could fall.

My vehicle seemed to be the only thing I could control, and when the pressures of life were on, I would find myself driving for hours. Driving was very therapeutic for me; I could relax and think, in fact, it was my only personal place where I had complete privacy.

But my dreams were crazy and big; sometimes I think too big for him. I was not afraid to dream big, for the Word of God was my motivation and my faith in Him allowed me to accomplish amazing tasks. I did not allow the fact that I had no high school diploma to hinder my goals.

My ability to effectively implement and govern the schematics of a growing school with no former training was an honorable victory. Scholars marveled at my accomplishments; many thinking I had gone to university to gain the knowledge I had attained. But my success was a direct result of following the plan of God for me. The reward for my obedience was an accumulated knowledge of teaching, directing and business planning.

In my particular sphere of activity, much wisdom was gained through experience. In the ten years of the school's operation, I proved that there was no limit to the possibilities. Regardless of my educational history, my desire to teach others caused me to soar over the standards placed by the education department. As a matter of fact, my students learned more efficiently than that of the overcrowded public school pupils and surrounding private schools.

As the school grew with my eldest daughter adding a new grade each year, I also grew. I stayed up numerous nights studying and preparing for the next day's lesson. I had found my niche in life; for I absolutely enjoyed what I was doing.

Eventually, my goal was to buy out all the private homes in my area. I would have the entire block designated as a community resource for education with the hopes of changing its street name to Noah's Ark Christian Boulevard.

But when a man violates the protective custody of his family, it is often seen in the life of his children. That is why God hates divorce; for it not only destroys the sacred union between the husband and wife but also dismantles and corrupts the order of God that was intended for the family.

Eventually, I would later discover that there was life after divorce and that my children did not have to be another statistic of divorced parents; dwindling downwards in the pessimisms of life. I resolved that I would not allow Satan to rob me of my future regardless of what he flung at me, but I also knew that my obedience was the key that would open the door to receive the promises of the kingdom. It would be the greatest challenge indeed.

The following morning, I dawned into a melancholic atmosphere with little energy. I had classes to teach, staff to greet and I was in no condition to see anyone. My husband and I met in the cellar where he held music classes for our students; that was the only other private place we could talk without any interruption. I cried and threw things around but as usual he never said much. I had been violated and betrayed; I left his presence feeling naked and ashamed.

As I left to clear my head, he gave me his cell phone and it was then that I recognized the name and number of the other woman. It was a very lonely day; I drove around for hours. When I finally reached home, it was late in the afternoon and all the students were gone. I was beside myself and very afraid of what lay ahead. I did not want to see anyone but nightfall was quickly approaching and it would be only a matter of time before the redundant sounds of the school bell would ring again.

God's Prophetic Messengers of Love and Mercy:
While I was preparing the next day's lesson for the substitute teacher, I got a call from my former assistant principal. He wanted to stop by. Over the course of the school year, he and his wife had become my personal friends and prayer partners.

We were introduced through a mutual friend when they both stopped by our school one sunny afternoon. He was also a principal of a Christian school, and I could see the satisfying look on his face as he got the grand tour. Not long after, he joined our team and enrolled his three children in our program; it was a successful school year.

Toward the end of the year, he finally informed us that he was relocating to Florida. Of course we were all saddened by the news; for not only was he an asset to the school, but he was a great friend too. He had caused the music department to double in its enrollment that year; we were all going to miss him.

I received a call from him that afternoon and he informed me that he was already on his way with his out town friend and wife who were visiting from Georgia. They were scheduled to leave the following day but according to them were instructed by the Lord to come by and visit with me.

As you can imagine, I was not in the mood to visit with anyone; let alone entertain strangers. But I quickly switched modes, prepared some drinks, and was ready to entertain. When I answered the door, the no make-up and no jewelry plain Jane but beautiful wife quickly revealed a bit of their Christian background. It did not matter though; I accepted and met people where they were. I had learned to get to know people by their spirit and not what they wore or didn't wear on the outside.

When asked how I was doing, as usual, I replied, *"Excellent!"* They sweetly smiled and sat down. As we began to make small talk, it didn't take long before the man of God revealed that he and his wife had specifically come to pray for me. I immediately took offense. Why would they think I needed prayer? I had not said anything to my friend, in fact, no one knew my dilemma.

Did they want to pray for me because I wore pants, make-up and jewelry or because they wanted to impose on me their religious do's and don'ts? For some reason, I thought they were about to argue about religion and Scripture, what you can eat or not eat, or what to wear and what not to wear. But I was in no mood to entertain such foolishness. Therefore, my walls of defenses shot up like gushing geysers and as the Jamaicans would say, *"I was finna blast dem."*

I knew they sensed my lack of enthusiasm and honestly, I didn't care. I was hurting and did not want anyone intruding or poking their nose into my personal business; let alone subject myself to unnecessary interrogations by some stranger. But they were very patient and took no offense to the many shots I fired from my three-sixteen and like two hunting cheetahs, they wasted no time to begin a scrutiny I found most offensive.

For those who know me, I had no problems being confrontational and blunt when necessary. However, this was by no means the time to be impolite and unthinking. My pride and hurt had blinded me from seeing that they were God's people. I failed to recognize that they were special agents sent to rescue me from a battle that had been purposely and personally waged against me. Thank God that He winks at our ignorance.

But as we engaged in conversation, I thought the pastor was off course when he asked me if I spoke in tongues. I snappishly replied that I did not know what that had to do with anything but he was persistent and asked a second time if I spoke in tongues. Agitatedly, I answered that I did.

When he asked me to speak in tongues I again inquired for what purpose. He rebuked me as he replied, *"You see, you are so full of pride that you can't even take instructions when a man of God tells you to do something. Now I said speak in tongues!"*

His authoritativeness almost broke me, but my overconfidence and contemptuous pride blinded me from receiving anything he had to say. I was more than agitated by now. How dare he command me to do anything, who did he think he was? I held my composure as I rudely retorted, *"Where are we going with this?"*

When he paused for a moment, the silence was so thick you could cut it with a knife. His wife just quietly sat behind the desk. I thought that if that had been me, I would have probably been all over me like white on rice. Nevertheless, she silently and patiently waited.

As he stared at the ceiling, I wondered what the heck he was looking at. Who was this man? I interrupted his thoughts and with one breath retorted, *"I'm sorry, I don't mean to be disrespectful. But every one here calls themselves a prophet and if you are a true prophet of God, then you better have my name and number and it better be correct. Because if you're not, as fast as you came in through my front doors that's how fast you're gonna leave."*

He broke into his unusual silence again and then said, *"God said to tell you that He wasn't the one who hurt you, but He apologies for the ones who did."* The anointing in his words immediately tore into my spirit. The power quickly disarmed the pride, fear, and mistrust that barricaded my fortified soul and hindered me from hearing and receiving the Word of the Lord.

I burst into tears as he again commanded that I speak in tongues. This time, I wasted no time to obey him because I knew that the Spirit of the Lord was in the house and right there in the room with me; I could feel His presence.

Another Vision of the Battlefield:

His wife knew it was her moment; she walked toward me, knelt down beside me and placed her arms around me and as I prayed in tongues she interpreted, *"Help me, help me Lord."* While I was yet speaking, I saw in a vision a battle. I was among many soldiers and on the frontline battlefield.

But in the midst of the combat, I came into view as being disoriented and very confused. I had been hit by a pipe bomb that the enemy hurled my way. For a brief moment, I was unable to act because I had taken a hit to the chest and the side of my head. Holding my head and clutching at my chest, I sought refuge behind some rocks. But the soldiers around me did not take notice that I had been severely wounded and was bleeding profusely.

Behind the rocks, I was able to regroup; it was there that I got a broader glimpse of the battle ahead. There was a war going on but most seem to be fighting their own personal battles. I observed soldiers that remained motionless as if nothing was happening. Did they not recognize the severity of the opposition we were up against? Some fought but many just stood around and watched as others tended to their personal wounds.

The negligent, daydreaming and unmindful disposition of the soldiers was no real threat to the adversary. The enemy did not bother them at all; interestingly, their only focus seemed to be on the soldiers that would not give up the fight.

Through bloody eyes, I looked on as one soldier lost her helmet. The enemy was brutally and viciously attacking her head, I could see the empty bald spots from where they had yanked out her hair. She was crying as she held to her head but she would not fight back. I yelled to her to run to the rocks but she just sat there crying.

I became angry as I yelled from behind the rocks at the ones who were at closer range; they did nothing but stare as if it were some circus side show. Their disposition left me bamboozled. If we were a team and on the same side, why were they not coming to my aid or the aid of the other girl who at the moment seemed to be in need of immediate attention?

I scuttled toward the soldier that had lost her helmet only to find her stretched out on the ground by the time I reached her. I could not tell if she was dead or alive but before I knew it, I heard the unleashing sounds of another pipe bomb. I saw soldiers taking cover and forgetting those that were left wounded on the battlefield and opened for further assault. I knew that I could not save everyone so I threw myself over her body; maybe just maybe she was still alive.

By now, I could see the enemy making ground and taking advantage of this opportunity. They went about slaying and plunging their swords into the soldiers that were left opened to the elements. Some were losing vital parts of their bodies; arms and legs were being cut off while others were having their eyes plucked out. It was a ghastly and grisly combat.

As I lay atop of the body, I could hear the breathing hums that whirred through her dried and crack lips. She was alive, thank God, she was alive! I told her that it was going to be okay and that I would get her to safety.

I dragged her mangled body across the ground and when the enemy saw me pulling her to safety, he darted my way. Forgetting the pain from the wounds I had sustained myself, I took one inflexible and fearless look at him and as we locked eyes, I screamed you cannot and will not have her!

He plunged full force in my direction but I steadily held to my place. My killer shoes anchored their pointed metal studs into the ground, giving me a secured and tenable stance. Making sure to stay focused on my target, I took out the lances in my belt and flung them as hard as I could; I knocked him straight off his feet and into a comatose state.

I beheld my comrades falling all around and the disconnection I witnessed within our unit infuriated me. Where was our task force commandeering plan of action? I looked through my binoculars to get a closer view.

With my listening device, I was able to hear captains arguing with their lieutenants about plans and strategies. They argued about whose plan was better and what was better, while others argued about the dress code, colors, insignias and things of no significance. No one was paying attention to the operation at hand. We were in a state of emergency and there was confusion and chaos everywhere.

But selfish and personal motives had found their way into the hearts of the company; every man for his own. The lack of unity, effective training, and inexperience added to the impediment of the company's mission. I noticed artless gunmen shelling ammo carelessly and wildly; dispatching bullets at anything that budged and occasionally causing injury to their own men.

Soldiers were unsuitably ranked and incorrectly titled into classes and groupings without proper preparation. The recruiting stations were full of hundreds of rookie soldiers with no experience, yet they were being thrown into combat.

I was told to survey, take notes and execute a written plan of corrective action of what I was about to see. How could I be asked to sit back and write in the middle of a raging war? I thought I should have been on the battlefield; they needed all the help they could get. But He who knew my thoughts gently replied that this was where I needed to be and what I needed to do.

I saw that we were suffering under the heavy setbacks of our own troops and I became very discouraged. I asked Him who knew my thoughts how we would win the war if our team was so off course and divided.

But I took note of a special defense group that appeared; they had large white stripe girdles that supported their upper and lower limbs. They were quite agile and swift as they moved around on the battleground like some *"cut-loose kicking butt ninjas."* They were competently and dexterously waging their swords with one hand and nimbly-fingered their shields to guard with the other. They were light on their feet and moved with supreme agility. I felt like I was watching an action packed adventure movie and all I needed was my sunflower seeds, a coke, and some popcorn.

But the majority of soldiers knew nothing about infiltrating their opponent's camp. Soldiers were carelessly falling into ditches and pits; many were completely oblivious to the traps before them and their inexperience on the battlefield caused many of them to lose their lives.

I was angry at the leading officers for imprudently sending inexperienced men and women into conflicts that should have been handled by the qualified veterans. How could they allow such a thing to happen? Soldiers were losing their lives trying to fight a war they did not understand. But I kept taking notes; carefully observing and writing all that I saw.

By now, the gashes and lacerations that I had suffered needed medical attention. I could no longer continue to doctor my wounds; they had become infectious and enlarged twice in size. I was in need of surgical treatment by a highly skilled, trained and experienced specialist.

I was wounded and knew if I didn't get help soon, I too would die just like the others had. Just then two comrades came into view; I could tell they were special agents because their uniforms were different from those of the common soldiers. They wore white with emblems of red stripes on their arms.

Back to God's Prophetic Messengers of Love and Mercy:

I was escorted away from the frontline of the battle

by these two agents. When I came to myself, I found myself broken and exhausted in the presence of the couple. They ministered to me for a while and when we were done, I apologized for my discourteous and boorish behavior. He replied that he was just as happy to leave with his head and face intact. Just before they left, they told me their last name was Battle!

I decided to meet with them again the next day but little did I know that I would undergo a Naaman's experience. Before further deliverance and healing could take place, the root of pride and its side-kicks would have to be dismantled and disarmed. I had allowed *Supercilious* to cause me to become a bigheaded smug. My first lesson in deliverance would begin with humility.

Chapter 14

Undercover

It was easy to give up my roots; in fact, I was more than happy to be finally rid of the old Puerto Rican, Narda Martinez when I married my Jamaican husband. I could not wait to sign my new last name on the dotted line. I would be rid of Narda Martinez **FOREVER**!

As I genuinely embraced the Jamaican culture, I steadily began losing further sight of the real me. Over the years, I would learn all about their traditions and way of life. I became a skillful impersonator and my affable simulations bamboozled just about everyone, particularly the Latinos and Jamaicans. My ability to follow their customs came naturally and I loved it. I was original, a specialist and there was only one me; the one and only, JamaRican, Narda Powell!

Although I blended culturally, my exotic features made it hard for people to define me. I was flattered when asked where I was from, not to mention the unusual accent I had now possessed. I cooked the food and understood and spoke the dialect "*patwah*" very well; I could even sing reggae songs. I loved the person I had evolved into and was finally accepted and admired by those around me. I felt protected and safe; celebrated among the people that had become my people, my teachers, mentors and spiritual leaders.

Over the years, I finally abandoned any recollection of my Latin-hood until I eventually was unable to connect with its way of life. I never knew when it was

Puerto Rican Day; the flags on the cars where my only indication. But when I heard Latin music, unwanted memories surfaced causing unspeakable throbbing in the deepest part of me. I did not have a handle on why I felt this way but I was determined that I would not permit myself to be wedged into the mudslides of despair once again; allowing her to increase would bring me back to a place of ignominy; a position of worthlessness and great personal humiliation. I vowed that I would never succumb to being vulnerable and susceptible to the attacks of being ME again. Therefore, Narda Martinez must remain hidden!

But the masquerade party was soon to be over. The clock stopped ticking; people gradually stopped convening. The show became boring and was no longer entertaining. There are no more masks to wear; no more pretenses, no more cloaks and concealing outfits to put on—no more hiding! Now I stand broken, naked and empty before my Lord.

Chapter 15

Judas Kiss

In the days ahead, my secluded and isolated world began closing in on me. I was lost for days as my hopes and dreams were shattered altogether. I couldn't shake the burdens that had now festered into a great mass. The empty feelings of the betrayal left me uncovered, naked and with gross feelings of shame and dishonor. I felt dirty and unclean. Although he said it had not gone further than a kiss, the Judas kiss left me very wounded; the end results were just as if he had gone all the way.

My dreams continued to torment me. I knew that if I did not find a way to release what I was undergoing, it would be only a matter of time before I'd suffer a severe mental breakdown—I began to write!

I kept everything I was undergoing a secret for a very long time but the anguish I carried as a result of his betrayal began to affect my ability to focus on my business tasks and personal ministry. The inner hurt was proving much more devastating than the legality of the marriage papers.

In the months that followed, our pastors began to wonder why we were taking so long to fix our legal issues. I had not yet disclosed his infidelity to them because I was too afraid of letting anyone know.

We finally took their advice and sought legal counsel from an attorney. She told us that we could do one of two things; annul the marriage or get a divorce and then remarry. I lost my composure when she mentioned the word divorce because I never believed in divorce. The truth of the matter was that I was faced with two options that were both equally terrible and I had to make a choice. I told her that I would rather annul than divorce; for some reason it seemed easier.

When the attorney saw how devastated I had become, she tried to convince me that it was not as bad as it appeared to be. She had seen things like this happen to others and that it was just a matter of repairing the paperwork. But the legality of the paperwork was not my greatest problem. My dilemma was overcoming the hurt I could not seem to escape.

In the weeks to follow, my husband appeared disinterested; almost as if he had forgotten all about it and in no rush to make things legally correct. As I watched the weeks turn into months, my fear was that with us not being legally married, in time, he would give up the fight to save whatever was left of the marriage; thereby making it easier to get out.

For a while things appeared to be going well. I thought we were communicating better as he would often tell me we were okay when I asked; giving me the security I needed. But the big puss I carried was becoming heavier each passing day and I knew that I needed to confide in my pastors.

One day, I decided to look through his phone bill. I discovered an old familiar telephone number that showed up quite often; too often if you ask me. I remember the panic I felt when I called him. Sensing the urgency in my voice, he made his way quickly to the house. I met him outside near the gate and told him it was the last time I would allow him to hurt me. As I ran toward the car, he grabbed me saying he was sorry.

When we got into the car, there was a dead silence. As he cried, the only words I could utter from my lips were, "I forgive you" and I meant it from the bottom of my heart. He looked into my eyes and said, "thank you" and then held me tightly as we both wept in each others arms.

I don't remember how long we cried but for the second time in my life, I was witnessing an emotional breaking on his part. I had only seen him vulnerable one other time— during his grandmother's funeral many years earlier. She raised him most of his life and he loved her very much. Therefore, her death affected him emotionally.

But I remember feeling like an outsider at the funeral as he cried holding on to his sisters and I looked on from a distance. I resented it for a long time because it was suppose to be my arms that he cried on. But in the car with him I remember thinking, he was now finally experiencing a real breakthrough into what seemed to be the hardest thing for him and yet what came so readily for me.

My spirit was crushed again but I loved my family and wanted to believe more than anything that we could weather the rocky storm of our marriage. He said he did not want a "divorce" and that the extent of his relationship with the lady was nothing more than mere conversations and that he had not slept with anyone. I believed in him and with the months passing away quickly, so did the old familiar number.

But soon my memory of the old familiar number was replaced by an alarming new one, for I had found another doubtful but consistent telephone number that was listed everyday. It caught my attention because the calls were initiated very early in the mornings and very late at night. When I confronted him about it, he became very angry and gave the excuse that she was a client who by the way had a husband and brushed it off as it being nothing more than that.

I was not convinced so I challenged him to call the number and place it on speaker phone. He dialed the number and when he realized that I was not bluffing, he closed his phone, got up and angrily walked out of the room. By now, I knew that we were not as "okay" as he had made me to believe. I thought that if he had nothing to hide then he would have appeased me by doing as I had asked.

Eventually, I got tired of the loneliness that I wallowed in day after day and I was exhausted from crying myself to sleep at night. I wondered what God did with all the tears that I cried because I had shed so many; then there were the anxiety attacks that struck me every time his cell phone rang. I had become a nervous and worrisome wreck. Not only had the betrayal gravely wounded my soul but it had legally opened a spiritual door causing me to fight demons I never had to fight before. The once confident and courageous woman that I had been known to be had now become desperate, jealous and insecure.

My wounds caused me to build bulwarks as high as the Berlin Wall and I trusted no one. To trust someone with my life meant exposing my very ugly bruises and risk the possibility of being let down again. Fear incapacitated my ability to see clearly and it was fear that blinded me from seeing two very special people God had placed in my life—my pastors!

But my pride had also become my greatest enemy. I had accomplished so much and had been unbeaten in pursuing my goals that I was more afraid of failing or being viewed as a failure. My marriage had been my greatest achievement and the one I took pride in above everything else. For years, we were a "model" couple. I was the strong Sister Narda who was always able to help people get out of their hole but now, I could not get out of the pit I had been so callously and unwillingly thrown into.

In spite of it all, reconciliation seemed very likely. He agreed to counseling and very soon afterwards, we opened up to our pastors at weekly sessions. We continued our routine of faithfully attending church with our family and things seemed to be getting better. He was still the drummer but by now I had stepped off the worship team. Our Pastor was teaching on marriage and relationship so we made certain to be present for them as well as any seminars and get-away retreats. By now he appeared to be doing everything he was supposed to do to make things right. With the type of teaching we were receiving from the pulpit and the one-on-one sessions, I had every reason to believe that we were on our way toward recovery.

The Prophetic Warning:

A year before the marriage physically fell apart, we had a prophet by the name of Cramer visit our church. As he ministered that afternoon, he was on point as he prophesied to every couple or person that was called up for prayer. When he got to us he told us that he saw a fight in the marriage arena and then turned to my husband and told him that the enemy had waved a carrot in front of him to lure him away. He was warn to pull away from the company he had been keeping and that if he did not, he would die by the end of that year. I could hear the hush as it shot through the congregation. People like to hear good prophesies and not the doom and gloom ones. But the prophet was not talking about a physical death but a spiritual one. It was a warning! He had received his warning from God.

You see, the Lord desires truth within the inward parts **(Psalms 51:6)** and before He passes judgment He sends a warning. According to His Word, what is in the darkness will always come to the light. Our relationship could not be healed because of his dishonesty. **Num. 32:23** says, *"be sure your sin will find you out."*

But my portentousness led me to reject the Word of the Lord that day and I complained to my pastors that although he had been on point with everyone else, he missed it when he got to us. I had allowed *Supercilious'* pompous attitude inveigle and influence my way of thinking which led me to believe that I always knew where my husband was and that he could do no wrong. Little did I know that the idol I had created of my husband and his image would come to a smashing end and a rude awakening to me.

Many people do not believe that prophets are for today. But Jesus denounced this mindset when He said in **Matthew 5:17** that He did not come to destroy the law or the prophets but to fulfill it. **Acts 3:25** says that we are children of the prophets and of the covenant which God made with our fathers.

Ephesians 4:11 lists the ministry gifts which Jesus Christ gave to his church. *"He gave some, apostles; and some, prophets; and some, evangelists; and some, pastors and teachers."* Jesus gave these gifts for equipping God's people for the work of service and for the spiritual growth and development of the body of Christ. If the ministry gifts were not for today, then they would not have been given to the church by the Lord.

The prophetic ministry dates back to the early church of our forefathers. The Old Testament prophets provide the framework (a beginning) for understanding the prophetic ministry. They spoke under the direct influence of the Spirit of God and their main concern was with the spiritual life and purity of the believer (the church).

The Old Testament prophets' main charge was to speak the Word of God in order to encourage God's people to remain faithful and true to their covenant relationship with Him.

Christ and the apostles serve as a paradigm of the New Testament ideal. Today, the New Testament prophet and his ministry operate very much like the prophets of old. New covenant prophets are empowered by the Holy Spirit to bring messages from God to His people (Acts 2:17; 4:8; 21:4). **The prophet is a Spirit-filled messenger and interpreter of the Word of God, that is called to warn, encourage, instruct, and comfort the body of Christ** (Acts 2:14-36; 3:12-26; 1 Cor. 14:3). **He is the recipient of God's revelation** (Rev. 22:6, 9) **and at times a seer who foretells future events** (1

Chr. 29:29, Acts 11:28; 21:10-11). He will expose sin, declare righteousness, warn of judgment to come and battle worldliness and lukewarmness among God's people (Luke 1:14-17). The prophet and his ministry will at times receive negative responses and rejection by many within the churches because of their message of righteousness.

But a prophet's message should never be regarded as infallible. They should be subject to the evaluation of other prophets, the church, and the Word of God (1 Cor. 14:29-33). The believer is always required to discern and test whether the prophet's witness is from God because there are many false prophets (1 John 4:1).

Prophets will continue to be essential to God's purpose for the body of Christ but a church that rejects God's prophets or prophecy will decline and drift toward the compromise of secularism instead of the Biblical truth and standards that are laid out in the Scriptures (1 Cor. 14:3, cf. Mat. 23:31-38; Luke 11:49; Acts 7:51-51). If the prophet is not permitted to bring words of forewarning and admonition and words that expose sin and unrighteousness (John 16:8-11), then the church will suffer the loss of the manifestations of the Spirit among the believers and become a place where the Spirit of the Lord can no longer be heard. When this happens, worldly influence and control will replace the working of the Spirit of the Lord thereby further plunging the church into lukewarmness and apostasy (2 Tim. 3:1-9; 4:3-5; 2 Pet. 2:1-3, 12-22). On the other hand, if the church heed and attend to the voice of God's prophets, it will be stimulated and inspired to grow in fellowship with Christ. Sin will be forsaken and the spiritual manifestations of holiness will be evident among his children (1 Cor. 14:3; 1 Thes. 5:19-21).

The Seduction of a Woman:

But deceit is like an infectious disease. It has the ability to attack its prey just like the strong jawed flesh-eating piranhas. It will gnaw and nibble at its victim until its flesh has been ripped, shredded and eaten; leaving nothing but emptiness.

I watched the life of a good man fall apart. He was a man that was known in the gates and one who sat among the elders (Prov. 31:23). Solomon witnessed something similar in **Proverbs 7:6-27**; the NKJV reads, *6 "For at the window of my house I looked through my lattice, 7 And saw among the simple, I perceived among the youths, a young man devoid of understanding, 8 Passing along the street near her corner; and he took the path to her house 9 In the twilight, in the evening, in the black and dark night. 10 And there a woman met him,* with *the attire of a harlot, and a crafty heart. 11 She* was *loud and rebellious, her feet would not stay at home. 12 At times* she was *outside, at times in the open square, lurking at every corner. 13 So she caught him and kissed him; with an impudent face she said to him: 14 "I have peace offerings with me; today I have paid my vows. 15 So I came out to meet you, diligently to seek your face, and I have found you. 16 I have spread my bed with tapestry, colored coverings of Egyptian linen. 17 I have perfumed my bed with myrrh, aloes, and cinnamon. 18 Come, let us take our fill of love until morning; let us delight ourselves with love. 19 For my husband* is *not at home; he has gone on a long journey; 20 he has taken a bag of money with him,* and *will come home on the appointed day." ²¹ With her enticing speech she caused him to yield, with her flattering lips she seduced him. ²² Immediately he went after her, as an ox goes to the slaughter, or as a fool to the correction of the stocks, ²³ till an arrow struck his liver. As a bird hastens to the snare, he did not know it* would cost *his life. ²⁴ Now therefore, listen to me,* my *children; pay attention to the words of my mouth: ²⁵ Do not let your heart turn aside to her ways, do not stray into her paths; ²⁶ for she has cast down many wounded, and all who were slain by her were strong* men. *²⁷ Her house is* the *way to hell, descending to the chambers of death."*

The Book of Proverbs chapter 7 warns men about the seducing woman. Sin is not bias and will cause us to commit the most heinous and scandalous crimes against those we love. The *Tempter's* mission is to ensnare and rob you of your blessings every time. Once you fall into his trap, he wheels you as his personal massive tool of destruction and then allows you to plummet in the heart of your own mess. You have no one to blame but yourself because the damage has been created by your own disobedience and willful rebellion. The fruit of it spawns into rotten augmentation that destroys and dispelled the light of God's love **(James 1:13-14).**

You do not recognize how far you have drifted away from the shores of safety until it is too late and you find yourself frail and weak in spirit. Like the prodigal son you are far from home and like Adam and Eve, you are forced to leave your once marvelous and beautiful garden; there are some things that we will not get a second chance at.

Chapter 16

My Perseverance at
Noah's Ark Christian Academy

Although the school was experiencing educational victories, we were facing financial difficulties. I was busy teaching and trying to keep up with the demanding activities that came with governing a growing school. I also taught combination classes of seventh to tenth graders. Teaching "combined groups" since the school's inception had caused me to master the direction and instruction of multiple groups with ease.

The next two years were particularly important to me. The school grew with our eldest daughter adding a new grade each year and I wanted more than anything for her to be the first student to graduate from **Noah's Ark Christian Academy**.

We were registered as a NYC non-public school and filing for the school's identification number with the state. Although we had our own testing system, this would allow our students to take the SAT's and Regents. A school is known in how well students score in these tests and it is what gives the school its credibility on a national and state level. By now, I was confident that both teachers and students had received a solid foundation in their training and education and that it was time for us to compete with the big dogs.

But new levels meant new devils, and it seemed that every time I took one step forward, the enemy would knock me two steps backwards. Our arguments soon led to threats of leaving, one night after an argument, he decided that he would sleep in a motel. I cried and cried as I tried to make him change his mind. I could not bear to stay in the house without him so I packed up some overnight clothing for the children and myself and we headed to a hotel in New Rock City. The children were delighted to go because New Rock City was their favorite place of entertainment. They were clueless as to what was really going on but I tried to keep my spirits up so that they would not suspect anything.

After they fell asleep, I found myself driving around for hours looking for him. I knew I could not baby-sit a grown man; it was too much work and too much gas. I suffered a long exhausting night.

When he came home the next day, he did not have much to say. I did not know what to do so I backed off and gave him the space he needed. But over the next two weeks, he found himself sleeping more often at the motel. It bothered me, but I knew I could not stop him. Up to that point, no one knew what we were really undergoing and that he had been gone because he was home early every morning fulfilling his usual routine around the home. But my staff could feel the tension when he was present and his van that was always parked in the driveway could no longer be seen. How long could I keep up the charade?

Then one week just before Mother's Day, I received a telephone call that changed the course of my life as I knew it forever. It was a beautiful spring day; some of the after-school students were outside playing basketball while I was on my upstairs porch working on my computer. You could hear the sounds of laughter and children running and playing.

It was normal for my husband to come in and out throughout the course of the day; sometimes he would forget a tool and have to come home. So on this particular day, I did not give it too much thought when he came home and rushed out without any explanation.

When I answered the phone, his faint and stuttering voice immediately troubled me. I knew that every time he started his sentence with *"we need to talk,"* he was about to throw a monkey wrench my way.

Fear gripped my heart as soon as he uttered the unbelievable words *"I'm not coming home anymore."* I braced myself behind my desk as he continued to say he needed time away. I could not believe what I was hearing. Had I been that blind to the truth of our situation?

After crying and pleading with him over the phone, he hung up and from that moment, I did not hear from him again. He rejected all calls and refused to return any messages from our pastors, trustworthy friends, the children or me. He had totally disappeared. No one knew where he was or where to find him. My music director who had been like a brother to us searched every hotel and motel in the Bronx while I looked through the yellow pages making phone calls after phone calls.

Finally, about four days later he decided to call, but by that time I was frantic and angry. I told him that although we had problems, deserting the children the way he had and refusing to acknowledge them by returning any of their calls was irresponsible and selfish. Of course, he thought I was preaching to him which made me very angry.

In the weeks that followed, he never returned home but frequently visited with the children and resumed to his normal duties. In August, he bought me a car so that I would be able to move around freely but when his vehicle was down, I would occasionally drop him off at his sister's house or at the presumed motel. I kept hoping that by the end of the ride, I would convince him to come home. But dropping him off was proving much more difficult every day and eventually he refused any more rides.

I knew that I was battling the principalities and powers that had now blinded his spiritual eyes. Many times, I could sense an uneasy demonic presence before he exited the vehicle. Sometimes, he would look at me and say he wanted to come home but just did not know how. He was trapped in confusion and the turmoil that now bound him slowly poisoned and desensitized his spiritual awareness.

I could smell evil lurking and the empty look in his eyes often led me to believe that I was not dealing with a full deck of cards. Even his physical demeanor began to change. The look of despondency was very evident; he did not shave or combed his hair like he used to. He appeared aloof, confused, discouraged, extremely bitter and angry most of the time; you would have thought I had been the one who cheated.

Sometimes, it led me to think that maybe it was my fault he was unhappy. I was willing to try anything, regain my coca-cola shaped body, cook more or possibly close the school. But eventually, I resolved that his unhappiness did not stem from me but from the unsettled issues he held in his heart. I could have been the perfect wife, did everything the way he wanted me to and he still would have been unhappy. He was somehow entangled in a web that could only be released by the power of the Blood of Jesus. Therefore, I kept praying for him.

In spite of the setbacks, we spoke for long periods during the night, and I remained optimistic and trusting that he would eventually face his demons and return home. I still opted to believe that he was being true to the covenant of our marriage because he said that his leaving the house had nothing to do with another woman. Then my pastor asked one day, "If he was not sleeping in my bed, whose bed was he really sleeping in?"

I continued to serve the Lord and attend church with my children. Because I no longer had a car, he took us to church every Sunday. But life was becoming very difficult because with no car, I felt like a sitting duck. It would only be a matter of time before we were left to take a taxi or arrange for a pick up because the person we had depended on the most was slowly making himself less and less available.

I was often concerned about his spiritual life and often prayed that he would find his way back to the Lord. He would not go to church with us anymore but he said he visited other ministries occasionally. He confessed that by the end of each service he was encouraged to return home but only to find that by the time he reached our block, a spirit of fear would overwhelm him, discourage and prevent him from doing what he knew was right.

What was it that he was so afraid of? Was it the guilt of failure that bound his mind? I could not get him to talk beyond the surface of his pain and finally, the evil that warred against his mind had strengthened to a point where he refused to receive any more reason.

Christmas 2005 in a New Home:

We had no private family life since the conversion of our home into a school, and the thought of a new home would provide that for us. Our home had become a public place of business with no escape from the frequent interruption; so a new home was ideal. By faith, I set sail in search of a new place to live.

It was around mid October that I told my spouse about the house I had found through a family friend. It was in New Jersey and about an hour and a quarter's drive from the Bronx. When I told the children they were extremely excited. They wanted more than anything to finally have a normal home with rooms they could call their own.

For six years, our beautiful home had been turned into a busy house that was full of rambunctious children. I sometimes felt like the old woman who lived in a shoe. The dining table was a combination of student desks we had put together and dressed up for special occasions or sit down dinners. Our beds were comprised of tri-fold daycare mats that we cushioned with blankets and pillows to remind us of the once upon a time comfortable beds we use to have. We had slept on blowup beds and daycare mats for so long, I think that we forgot what a normal bed felt like. But it was all in the name of securing a better future for our children. I was fulfilling my passion in life and the inconvenience was temporary. The goal was to make enough money to purchase a second home while still governing the growth of the school.

It was a cold and rainy night as we drove the lengthy roads of I-95. The extremely dark atmosphere and wetness of the roads made our journey a lot longer, but the rain had dwindled by the time we pulled into the stretched driveway. There were many trees, a mansion two houses down, and a beautiful lake across from the house.

A nice young man greeted us at the door. He was very cordial yet professional as he gave us the grand tour. The house had enough rooms and bathrooms to accommodate a family of five. It had a beautiful fireplace in the living area, a game room, a library room, a sunroom that was filled with exotic plants and what I have wanted mostly in a home—a swimming pool! I was sold the moment I saw it. It was not my dream home but anything was better than living where we were.

We decided to accept the terms of renting with the option to buy and he agreed to pay for the mortgage. As we moved in the beginning of December 2005, I was hoping that the new house and the fresh surroundings would afford us with the privacy we needed as a family. I stayed very hopeful and sense that it was a good move and that he would join us soon.

The extremely quiet area that was very much different from the city life was going to take some getting use to. Occasionally, you would see one or two people walking their dogs or a child riding his bicycle but since it was winter time, there wasn't much activity happening. When I took a stroll around the neighborhood, I noticed that most people did not have shades or curtains in their windows and you could see just about everything that went on inside their homes. Of course, I was not use to this sort of openness. The overpopulated city I came from was an action-packed thriller with many daily adventures; some good, some bad.

The windows in our private homes were completely different from the ones in our new surroundings. Our windows contained decorated bars of steel to keep the intruders from breaking in, plus shades and curtains which most people never opened. To add to this, the security locks and bolts on the doors used cost a fortune. It was like living in jail, and in case of a fire, you had better remember where the key to that window was or you were going to fry. It made me mad to think of the amount of money we had to spend to live in a shoebox with window guards. Have you ever played the game Monopoly only to land on Park Avenue or Boardwalk? God help you if a player of that space had houses or hotels on it; one time on it would be enough to bankrupt you.

But this Christmas was not as magically enchanting like the ones we were used to years before; I decided to decorate and liven up the place anyway. With beautiful decorations and the sounds of Christmas music in the air there was still an empty feeling in the house. His presence made a big difference and we really missed him. While the children liked the house, they did not like being so far away from the city and their friends and often cried to go back to the Bronx.

On Christmas Day, the girls and I could not wait to see him. I cooked dinner early and set the table very pretty. Time stood still as we anticipated his arrival. When he finally came through the door, I could feel a tension between us as I greeted him with a kiss. We were both nervous around each other; almost as if we were strangers meeting for the first time.

The girls gave him their gifts and you could hear the sounds of talking and laughter that echoed from the rooms. When we got our chance to talk, I asked him if he would be joining us soon and he said "maybe." With our new environment and an actual home to come to after work, things were looking hopeful for us after all.

Back to the School:

But our first day commuting back to school, I got into a car accident and damage the car he had just bought a few months earlier. We did not have the extra money to pay for the repairs immediately so that restricted us to living back at the school until I was able to get another vehicle.

For years, my home in the Bronx had also been my workplace; one could say that I never left home and that I never left work. The last thing I saw when I went to sleep was a chalkboard and it was also the first thing I saw when I woke up every morning along with the sound of the loud and annoying school bell. But my youngest daughter could not wait for the holiday break to be over and return to school. While she considered commuting back and forth a luxury the other students had, the other kids thought quite the contrary and said she was the lucky one. Living at Noah's Ark had its advantages. During the winter months when snow was incredibly a great deal, I did not have to worry about the hustle and bustle of being late for work, traffic or the parking issues that most people encountered. I just rolled out of bed and I was there. But along with many of the advantages came a lot of discomfort and sacrifices.

The Longest Night… Truth about the Other Woman:

This would be the night that would finally push me over the edge. That evening my heart was once again place under tremendous strain when he called and said we needed to talk. I was as nervous and sick as the first day he told me about the marriage. He was not much of a talker but when he did talk, it usually left me with the carpet pulled from under my feet. **I could sense he was about to unearth something terrible so I braced myself for the big blow**. He then uttered the unbelievable words I had heard before but this time it was bringing a much more devastating aftereffect. It was no more sleeping at hotels and no more pretending.

Scared of knowing the answer, I took a deep breath and asked if it had anything to do with another woman and he finally said it did. I asked him how long he had he been unfaithful and he dispassionately answered three years. I was mortified as his report left me in total disbelief and broken. I begged him to rethink it over and pleaded for him to call Pastor Mott. He said he did not want to talk anymore and hung up the telephone.

How could he walk out of my life and the life of our children just like that? He meant the world to me. He could not possibly end it like this or could he? I could feel the pain flooding my heart as the old yet familiar spirit of abandonment and rejection swiveled a sardonic pirouette. How was I going to tell the girls that their daddy who had been known as our hero for so long was not coming home anymore? I wanted to protect them as much as possible.

It was hard enough having to deal with my pain but the pain that was about to be unleashed into their little hearts added to my calamity. I frantically paced back and forth and cried, *"The children, my God, the children!"* But even though he had hurt us, I could still feel love in my heart. I wanted to turn it off like a faucet but I could not; for I couldn't see my life without him.

When I walked into the hallway, I found the eldest daughter standing there. The others knew something had gone terribly wrong for my pleading cries over the phone were heard from the other side of the room. I could feel my body shivering from the fear that absorbed my heart like a wet sponge. I gazed into her beautiful tiny eyes and found that they too were filled with panic and fear. I knew I could not hide it anymore and trying to find the right words to tell her about her daddy was a heart wrenching task.

I had never heard her cry the way she did that day. She marched back and forth in distress crying, *"Mommy, what are we going to do, what are we going to do?"* I'll never forget the sound of the cries that echoed from the others in the room. The home that had been known for so much love, laughter and joy had now turned into a house of overflowing sorrow and grief.

But I became angrier by the minute as I thought what a selfish coward he had become. All he could think about was his unhappiness; well what about mine? He wasn't the perfect husband with all the right moves either, yet I had learned to live beyond the disappointments of my spouse. I was a big social butterfly who loved the ambiance of fine dining, romance, dancing and other social activities while he on the other hand was the complete opposite and would be just as content with a home cooked meal, a television and a newspaper. I had resolved that even if he didn't change, I would still love him. Then there was the most important thing we had in common; our children. I do not think he ever thought about the damage he would inflict on them.

I thought about the many opportunities I had to commit adultery. But the smooth talking and flattery of men or the sophisticated, wealthy Lotharios I encountered in my time could not move me from my place. I knew who I was as a child of God but I also knew that if I took my eyes off Jesus, I would found myself in the same position. There wasn't much to think over because the consequences that infidelity would inflict on my family just wasn't worth it; plus, I loved them too much.

I knew I hadn't been the perfect wife, but who is? Nothing in life is a one hundred percent, but if I had to rate myself as a woman, wife and mother out of the hundred percentile, I would give myself a big round of applause eighty.

The enemy causes us to think that the twenty percent that's lacking in our lives is much greater than what we already have. When we murmur and complain about what we don't have, we fail to recognize the blessings we do have. Many that have left families, spouses, and churches for the measly twenty percent eventually find out that the grass isn't always greener on the other side, and when they get there, they realize that the grass will need cutting and weeding too. When people reject you and tell you that you are not enough, know your worth and as T.D. Jakes plainly put it one day; just say, *"Eighty-twenty baby"*.

The fact that I was able to govern the temptations of self-pity and neglect that I often felt as a wife, I did not allow the lame excuse of not receiving attention or the dissatisfaction of my spouse govern my actions. I was infuriated when I thought about the commitment and sacrifices I made as a woman, a wife and mother. I could not help but feel cheated and that life had dealt me a bad hand.

In desperation, I called his phone but he continued to ignore them. I would redial for long periods until I got tired and frustrated and finally threw down the phone. To add to our grief, our family dog of about twelve years died that night. He was what I would call a man's best friend. Oh, how he loved that dog. But his spiritual decline had allowed the enemy to engross his way of thinking. The abandonment of his household, marriage and fatherly duties was the physical manifestations of a man whose spiritual life was no longer led by the Spirit of God. His refusal to repent, obey and separate himself from all compromise had finally led to his spiritual darkness **(Luke 11:34-35).**

That night, my pastors hurried over to our house, but my husband's refusal to respond to urgent messages left by them had confirmed his spiritual condition. You could see their looks of concern and disappointment. They had poured so much into our lives through prayer, the pulpit and the one-on-one sessions.

The Lighted Candle:

Luke 11:33-36 speaks about the parable of the lighted candle. When a person's spiritual eyes are directed toward the will of God, the light of His Word enters into his spirit resulting in the promises of the blessing of Psalms 1. But, if his desires are not focused on the things of God, then darkness will triumph and the revelation of God's truth will have no effect. We are cautioned to resist the devil at all times and he will flee **(James 4:7).**

But when a believer fails to completely renounce and forsake the sin in his life or open his life to the Spirit of God, he is inviting a life of compromise and proper discernment and sound moral judgment will eventually be lost. Disobedience always leads to spiritual decay, and as believers, we must always be on the alert and commit ourselves to radical obedience to Christ, righteousness, prayer and the Word **(Romans 8).**

We need to understand that Satan's power does not end after our conversion to Jesus Christ. He will forever serve as a never-ceasing menace whose main goal is to bewitch us to disobey the Truth **(Galatians 3:1)**. His self-assigned job is to seek and destroy.

The story of Samson is another example of those believers who think that God will remain with them even while they continue in sinful, immoral and dishonest behavior. Samson's first mistake was a total disregard of God's instruction to remain separate from the wicked nations of the Canaanites which by the way, eventually influenced him to enter into compromise with Delilah **(Deut. 7:1-4).**

Flirting or playing with sin over a period of time will desensitize you to righteousness. Compromise will always open up one's life to the power of Satan, delusion and in due course to utter defeat. **Delilah which means languishing** on three occasions tried to obtain the secret of Samson's strength. She pressed him continually until she got him to yield. But he never realized that his infatuation with her would ultimately cost him his sight as he gradually fell into a spiritual slumber.

He failed twice to recognize that he was being set up by the enemy. But after the third account, he was so spiritually sedated that he was totally unaware of his present condition when the enemy came in to arrest him. He had not realized that the Lord had departed from him due to his continual disobedience **(Judges 16:20).** He thought he could pursue his enemy as in times past only to find that the presence of the Lord had departed. Compromise will snuff out the light of God and cause us to stumble in darkness.

If you notice, the first physical thing done to Samson when he was captured by the Philistines was that his eyes were put out **(Judges 16:21). He had become blind; a physical manifestation of his spiritual condition. He went from being a judge in Israel to a blind prisoner in the grinding mill. To add to the humiliation, they made a public sport of him.** It is the enemy's will to ultimately parade you in open degradation and dishonor.

His obsession with Delilah, her deceitfulness and his melancholic death should serve as a reminder that those who willfully disobey will languish in utter defeat. But thank God that this poignant story did not end here. Samson cried out to the Lord and his prayers were answered

(Judges 16:28). God's grace is always available to those who truly repent from the heart **(Ps. 51:17).**

The Car Chase:

I recognized that my fight was not with another woman. She was merely a tool that Satan used to bring the man of God to a compromised state. I was not the first woman to be betrayed by a man and I would not be the last. My battle was with the enemy of my soul who had once again found a way to forge his evil vendetta against me.

But I had yet to learn the valuable lesson of mastering my emotions and in the days ahead, I became enslaved to my flesh and the victim to an emotional roller-coaster fiasco from hell. I did not sleep that night and early that morning, I decided to give him a call. It was not over as far as I was concerned. I still had many unanswered questions.

He continued to ignore my calls for about half an hour when I somehow intercepted his call. In the background, I could hear the familiar sounds of a loud speaker which indicated he was in Home Depot. When he realized that I was on the other line, he refused to talk and hung up the phone again. By now, I was irate and extremely agitated and decided to make my way to Home Dept. I took my eldest daughter with me in hopes that her presence would keep me from doing anything irrational and crazy; but everything would turn out to be less than peaceful that morning.

By the time I got to the parking lot, I was ready to slash his tires and bust out all his car windows. But when I spotted his car, I decided to wait. I quickly trailed up and down some of the isles and spotted him as he was at the counter checking out his goods. Angrily I shouted, *"Hey, you!"* I then proceeded to use a couple of choice words I am too embarrassed to mention. You could see the look of fury on his face when he saw me. I wanted to talk and he did not. But I was hysterical and the fact that he treated me like a worthless nobody enraged me all the more. I was the mother of his three children and his wife of sixteen years and all he could say was go home?

By now I had created a scene. I was crying, screaming and yelling at him and in a violent frenzy swung my little Coach purse at him. He threw down the packages he held in his hands when he saw the purse coming and charged at me like a raging bull. The hateful look in his eyes told me he was going to kill me. He grabbed a hold of my chest and with all his might flung me onto the concrete floor.

As I came slamming down to the ground, I held on with all my might taking him down with me. Disoriented and hurt from the fall, I could not believe that this was the same man I had loved so much. In the years we had been together, he had never physically harmed me. But I was now frightened as I beheld the possessed look in his eyes. Who was this man? Certainly not the loving father and husband I had married. Something evil had now overtaken him and I was afraid that I had lost him forever.

I tried to struggle free from under him only to find myself pinned under his weight. I was screaming and telling him to stop and to let me loose but he clutched at my neck as if to choke me and with that came an unexpected blow to my face.

I was furious as I jumped to my feet and headed toward his car. With all my might, I took one swing at his car window shattering glass everywhere. I stepped toward the next window to do the same when his long legs darted in my direction. I could hear our daughter crying and screaming at us to stop. It was a horrible scene at the Home Depot's parking lot that morning but I did not care if anyone saw or recognized me. I wanted him to hurt just like he had hurt me.

By now, men had gathered around to protect me from the avenging onslaught that was coming my way. Cut, bruised and bloody from the fight, I was taken to my vehicle. My fingers and hands were badly bruised and sprained but I finally managed to start the car.

But just when you thought it couldn't get any worse, think again. I was emotionally declining fast. I had permitted my unbalanced emotions to lead me driving up and down the streets in a confused and obsessed mental state.

Eventually, I caught up with him. As he was entering into his car, I pulled up beside him. It was evident that he was through when he brushed me off again and backed up to pull out, but I quickly backed up my vehicle and blocked him in. We went backwards and forwards in this manner until finally I let him out.

I followed behind him hoping he would eventually pull over but instead it turned into a hot pursuit. We ran through red lights and stop signs and occasionally, I would bang the back of his bumper with my car.

I then noticed that he was on his cell phone. Who could he be talking to at a time like this? When I thought he was calling the police, we finally stopped in front of Sean's house; he was our spiritual brother and also one of our leading musicians. It did not take long before the bushy long haired, tall and slender young man who I love so much walked into the street where we were. Before he could get close to my vehicle, I told my daughter to get out of the car. I did not want to endanger her life anymore than I already had. By now, I knew I was losing all sense of my sanity and good sense but I could not stop myself. My careless and thoughtless acts were wheeling me out of control and things were getting worse.

He approached my vehicle and calmly tried to convince me to pull over. But the desperation to hold to my world that was slipping from my fingers by the minute impaired my ability to listen to any reasoning.

I could hear Sean's words fading away as I remained focused on the vehicle before me. I knew him well and my quick thinking prevented his swift attempt to get into the car. But the distraction had now afforded my spouse the opportunity to take off. As I attempted to take off behind him, he stepped in front of the car to prevent me from following. I screamed at him to move out of my way and jerked the car in a forward motion and he quickly moved.

I eventually caught up with him and we began to circled around locally again. His maneuvers to shake me on the road only caused me to stay focused and dead on his tail; I think he had forgotten that he had taught me how to drive. When he headed toward the highway, I buckled up my seatbelt. I was ready for the long haul and was not going to allow him to get away so easily.

Not long after, I noticed that he was on his phone again. Maybe this time he was calling the cops. After all, I did bust out his car window, whacked the back of his car and now was in a hot pursuit after him on a major highway. It was a miracle that we didn't get stopped for speeding or reckless driving.

When he exited at an odd but familiar exit, I trailed closely behind. We proceeded onto an industrial area parallel to the highway and there he pulled into a busy gas station and parked at an angle. His position marked a speedy getaway, so in turn I parked myself in a reckless slant that blocked both sides of traffic. It was the only position that would permit me to take off in any direction in case he sped off again.

I could hear the sounds of motorists tooting their horns at me and the occasional shouts of people screaming as they looked on in bewilderment. But it did not matter anymore because I was now engrossed with a raging passion that was hungry and out for revenge.

As unwholesome thoughts flooded my mind, I felt like ramming my car into his side. Time stood still as the outside voices and sounds of cars slowly faded. My flesh and spirit went to war as I contemplated my next move. But then, a clear and authoritative voice interrupted the subterranean thoughts that were drowning me, and it said, *"Narda, park the car!"*

I followed the voice only to find Raymond, my music director, standing in the middle of the road. It was like he had magically appeared out of nowhere. He had been a brother to me since the age of fifteen and over the years our families had grown very close. But there he was in the middle of road. It was like Scotty had been beamed him down from the Star Trek spaceship.

I finally replied that I would quit and go home if he would only talk with me. As he backed up toward the other car, he never took his eyes off me. They exchanged words and then he slowly made his way toward my direction. I heard the commanding words again, *"Narda, park the car!"*

Captivated by the tone in his voice, I answered back, *"Two reason why I'll park the car; one because it's you and two because it's your car."* But it was more than the car just being his; I trusted him and the anointing on his life. I believe that it is for this reason that the Lord sent him. After all, it was he who had loan me the car.

The Altar:

My head hung low as he entered the vehicle and sat beside me. I was exhausted and overwhelm in heartache. With a compassionate look and a mellow tone voice, he asked if I wanted him to drive. That was just like Raymond, usually calm, cool and collected. He did not yell and scream or say any of the things I assumed he would say considering what had just happened.

We switched sides and as we started off, I could hear his voice fading in and out. I had lost all sense of direction and time and nothing seemed familiar to me anymore. All I could feel was the throbbing sting of the betrayal and the loss.

The unpleasant and sickening feeling that engrossed my mind left me believing I was dirty and unclean. I could not help but tear at my clothes in frenzy as I told him that I needed a bath. I wanted to scrub the filth I felt inside of me. My world was spinning out of control and I thought I was losing my mind. I don't recall if the car was moving or parked but when I attempted to open the car door, the force of his hand restrained me. He promised to take me to a place where I could shower.

We pulled up at his mother's house and there he sat me on the living room floor. I do not know how long I had been there, but I was grieving over my loss. I felt like I was at a funeral and someone had died that day.

After all that had taken place, I knew that I needed to talk with God. I could not continue on the declining emotional slope of no return. What I had been through had scared me. I had lost my composure in God for a split second and if it was not for His grace, my choices would have allowed the enemy legal grounds to destroy my life forever. I asked him to quickly get me to the church altar.

Chapter 17

Living with Rejection and Abandonment

It was about two weeks before we heard from him and in the following months he would disappear for weeks at a time. We were left with no vehicle, no money and debts that had sky rocketed. How could he have allowed the enemy to use him to bring such dishonor to our family name and the God we had been serving for so many years?

But I kept calling and leaving endless messages and eventually, I would see him pull up in the familiar silver car. The driver always parked away from the house as if not to be seen. He would the drop the money into the mailbox and then take off.

I began to retreat behind walls to seek the remoteness I felt inside. No longer did I enjoy the things I used to do. My children could not understand why I would shutter the windows while it was yet daytime. During the evening, I made them find their way around the house without having to turn on many lights. I asked them to walk softly and rebuked them when they spoke too loudly. I don't know what I was fearful of, but I did not want anyone to know we were home alone. By five o'clock, I made my way for bed as if I were hiding from someone or something.

The melodies of a harmonious and joyful spirited home could no longer be heard. The laughter and singing had now turned into sorrow and much sadness lingered. Our safety and comfort had now turned into panic and fear.

Friends were no longer able to visit, neither were the children able to enjoy an afternoon on the front porch as was our routine. My eldest daughter did not understand the severity of my depression and would often ask *"Mom, what's wrong with you!"* What would we do and what would become of us?

On one occasion when he came to visit the girls, our lights had been turned off for about two weeks. He did not stay long and as he was leaving, *I said to him that wherever he was laying his head at nights, I hope he felt good to know he could turn his lights on and off.* I then proceeded to demonstrate by flipping my switch. Obviously, the lights did not turn on which was the point I was making. I did not know how he could sleep knowing that he had left us in such depraved conditions. But everything was coming down to a crashing end very quickly.

As time passed the electricity was turned off again several times for nonpayment. I had no idea that the water and property taxes on the home were overdue and that the city had taken a lien against the house. To make matters worse, I was left to contend with the mortgage company; something I knew absolutely nothing about. We were soon to lose the only house we had which meant I would lose the only means of supporting my children and me. Needless to say, we continued to fall further behind in our bills.

I was battling so many obstacles at one time that becoming bitter was proving to be very easy. The desertion of his financial support and demands that were outstanding left me dwindling from month to month because he was not contributing to our family anymore.

His lying, cheating and failure to communicate truthfully had finally put an end to our marriage.

With no prior experience in dealing with finance and mortgage companies, I did not know what to do. Thank God that one of my students had parents who were involved in real estate and they did not hesitate to come to my aide. I was able to refinance the house and save us from losing our home. I must confess that today, I still don't know how I managed to pull it off, but all the glory goes to God.

Chapter 18

Where Are You?

My memories of Narda Martinez are full of pity. I do not recall great accomplishments or major victories. All I remembered are failures, misfortunes, many disappointments and a wish that I had never been born. Why should I care about her now? It is twenty odd years later.

The stripping of each layer is crushing as God began to unfurl the deep places in my life. My heart panted with fear as we began to walk through the corridors of my wounded-heart. I did not want to have another look at the ache of rejection for it was too painful. The revisit of this old, yet familiar place was like pacing through an obscure antechamber. As I approached closer, I could hear the echoes of fury and the bellowing sounds of a weeping child, the unrelenting silence of an unhappy little girl who was abandoned, rejected and left to survive on her own. I was now forced to face my greatest fear— **ME!**

Everything in me wanted to run and hide. Nothing in me wanted to reflect on the times yore. If I had my own way, I would run far, far away. *Oh, that I had wings like a dove, for then I would fly away and be at rest; but then, I would wander off and remain in the wilderness* **(Psalms 55:6)**. But if I was to fulfill my destiny, it was imperative that I die to self and allow the crushing to take place. I had to open the door and allow the *Savior* to enter my secret place, a place where monumental phantoms had claimed territory. No one had ever entered here, for I had this place barricaded, restricted, and concealed. Only I knew this place existed or so I thought, but the time had come to revisit this forbidden and unwelcoming site.

God's Vision of the Real Narda Martinez:

As we began the tour, I took a fleeting look into several rooms and saw old familiar dusty pictures and memoirs. I hastily shut the doors and scuttled through the halls not desiring to remain any longer than I needed. I entered the corridors only to pass a shrouded goddess, who cynically hissed and odiously attacked my self-esteem. She cruelly whispered, *"Who do you think you really are?"* I took a deep breath and with my head held up, I retorted, *"A daughter of Zion!"*

As I continued across the threshold, my attention was drawn to the disheartening sounds coming from the room way down on the other side of the hallway. As I got closer, just behind the doors, I could hear a child weeping. I did not understand why she had been crying until I peered through the cracked door and saw that she had been at play with her dollhouse. Someone had deliberately and maliciously overthrown her beautifully put together dollhouse. All the pieces had been precisely positioned in their respectable spaces but were now in disarray and scattered all over the room. Who would callously plot to destroy her perfectly designed dollhouse? I left her crying with her arms folded across her chest and feeling sorry for her.

As I entered through another passageway, I came to a room teemed with mirrors. They were all colors, shapes and sizes. Each piece had been skillfully and beautifully handcrafted and each had its own peculiarity. But the mirrors troubled me because I knew they reflected something that I was not ready to face, so I quickly shut the door.

Chapter 19

Buried But Not Dead

I thought I had perfectly buried this place. I was certain I left no memorials or landmarks for recognition or identification. I kept no record of the gradual self-inflicting death that I had imposed upon myself. But God knew and He knew it all.

The self-slaughter had continued for years. I never realized that in the process of hating, resenting and suppressing who I really was, I was also destroying the very person my husband loved and treasured. I had no idea that what I had done was to my own demise. I had no knowledge of the pain I inflicted upon him, nor how I made him undergo the suffering of watching the woman he cherished so much die a slow and ongoing death.

But God began to visit the deep places of my soul. He paced through the corridors of my heart, each time hitting me like a tsunami and destroying everything that was unlike Him in its path. He was searching, finding, pulling, breaking, tearing and clearing out all the debris that had taken root over the years. He touched my broken areas; pieces that were only patched and appeared to be whole and issues I could not face up to on my own. This was unfair and unjust. How could a loving God that said that He loved me permit what had taken place? He knew before I got married what would happen. Why would He allow me to suffer this tragedy? What glory could He get from all of this?

But if I were to be used by Him, this broken vessel would need inner healing and a release from a spirit of rejection and self-hatred that dwelt in the inner chambers of my heart. I had carried this load for years and my deliverance had come; yet it was not coming without a fight.

This was the time in my life when it looked like it was the end of the road, the end of my dreams and the end of me. Although my problems were greatly stacked against me, I knew that in my own strength, I was no match for life's problem. The biggest fight of my life was on and it was a battle to outlast the thoughts of my wounded past. Now, I had to focus on what was left and not what was lost. I knew that Satan had gone before God and made his accusations against me, just as he had done with Job. I was having a real "Job experience."

Warning: *If you are serious about being used by God, you will have a "Job experience," you will have to confront Goliath and encounter times of depression like Elijah. You will ultimately face Gethsemane whether you want to or not.* What you do with your battles and challenges is up to you.

But warfare had been declared, and although the saints of God were under girding me, it was my fight. It was as if my spiritual brothers and sisters had now stepped behind the sidelines. As Pastor Connie plainly put it one day, *"I had fifteen brothers and sisters, out of which ten were boys. One day, I had to fight a bully in school and my brothers had warned me that if I didn't fight the bully, they were going to give me a beating; and if I fought and lost the fight, the beating would be doubled.* The day of the fight, she exclaimed, *'Everyone gathered around,'* and one of my brothers pulled me out from behind the skirts of my siblings and yelled, *'Now go kick her butt!'* And that I did!"

As she told the story, she skipped around as if she were a boxer in a boxing arena. I was motivated as this older woman of God passionately and tenaciously sermonized words of encouragement into my life. I left her presence that evening full of the power and strength of the Holy Ghost.

But the immediate battle was becoming uncomfortable and disheartening; and as soon as I got home that evening, the combat was on. I was viciously bombarded with negative thoughts and I knew I had to immediately gear up for combat and waged war over the strongholds that aimed to inundate my mind.

I remember my nights being the worst of all. For it was then, in the stillness of the night that loneliness would uninvitingly cuddle its poisonous arms around me. His undesirable comrades made themselves my bedroom guest every night. I dreaded the nightfall because it only reminded me of the rejection and abandonment I felt.

Every night they arrived with their tormenting and venomous sonata, enslaving my mind to their ghastly-oeuvre in order to spellbind my already crestfallen soul. Their luring symphonies interlaced my thoughts and inveigled my judgment. Each time I was consistently led to a place of desolation where I would wallow into the hopeless lake of despondency; there unrelenting distress and sorrow subjugated every part of my soul.

Many times I felt pressurize to concede defeat. I grew tired of the importunate opposition I faced day after day. But the more the enemy dished out, the more I flexed and wielded my Sword. I had come too far and I knew I could not back down. There was too much at stake and victory was contingent upon my fortitude. So through clouded tears, serrated trails and daunting courses, I prevailed against the melancholic fabrications my adversary hurled my way while each time fixing my eyes on the prize ahead.

Chapter 20

Fight the Good Fight of Faith!

My pastor's punctilious teaching of the Word of God brought me much clarity on wholeness and the fulfillment of my destiny. The *Words of Life* he ministered became the very words that I had to regurgitate throughout the caterpillar stages of my life. These truths preserved me during my time of distress and as the plan of God began to unfold, I soon realized that the trials I encountered in the earlier stages of my life were lessons orchestrated to prepare and teach me the life skills I needed as a soldier.

My position as a believer was to overcome every obstacle, defeat every trial, outweigh every burden and endure every hardship that came my way no matter the cost. **Ephesians Chapter 6** plainly puts it, **"having done all to stand."**

How could I successfully minister to others if I had not dealt with my own issues? I was tired of putting on the masks and pretending that everything was "okay." Everything was not "okay." In fact, my world had just collapsed and there was not anything that I could do to change it. I needed strength to accept the things I could not change, courage to change the things I could and the wisdom to know the difference—the good ole Serenity Prayer.

Christians can put on the biggest facade. We have the most inspirational speeches and smoothest dance moves. But our titivating fashion should lead us all the way to the Oscars for being the most illusive leading actors.

How could I help a dying world if I was not willing to be honest about my own issues? I was still gravely wounded, hurt and angry and before I could minister to others, I knew that I needed to be truly healed, delivered and set free. Otherwise, I would be functioning as a false prophet by telling others to receive something I myself had not.

But issues caused me to hit a wall every time and unless I confronted them they would forever hold my soul in captivity. Until I face up to them, they would continue their never ending mockery of my private humiliation.

I am so grateful that my Savior, Jesus Christ understood my humanity. He was a fulltime partaker of the human race for thirty-three years. It is evident in **John 3:16** that the Father has not requested anything from us that He himself has not fulfilled.

While Jesus was a faithful servant to everyone He knew, one who had walked closely with him betrayed him with a kiss and thirty pieces of silver. And in Gethsemane, when He needed His closest friends the most, they fell asleep on Him; He knew first hand what loneliness, rejection, abandonment and treason felt like. Jesus was the first partaker of what He preached and a true prophet. As you read His life story, you may find yourself relating to many of his encounters.

Christianity does not exempt one from having personal issues. Our problems do not magically disappear as most people would like us to believe. Christians need continual deliverance from the hurts and wounds of the past, in addition to, healing from the existing issues at hand.

Several women in the Bible had personal issues and so will you and I. Let us take into the account the Shunamite woman and the death of her son (death and loss of a loved one), the Samarian woman who had many husbands (a woman who slept around), Sarah and the mistress (marital problems and that **miss** was **stress**). Then you have the woman with the issue of blood (health problems), Esther and her inter-racial marriage, and Ruth and her mother-in-law (hers happened to be a *blessing*). Then there are the men and their problems, like Abraham and the other woman, Elijah and his suicidal issues, the prophet Hosea and his harlot wife, David the murderer and adulterer, handsome Samson and his flirtatious ways, and the list goes on and on.

We must come out of denial and stop hoping that wishful thinking will dissipate our hurts. We must come boldly before God with great expectations **(Heb. 4:16)** and trust that He will give us the answer or the strategy for overcoming every situation. But on the other hand, if we continue to ignore and pretend that these issues do not exist, we will be like that man or woman that looks into the mirror and walks away forgetting what manner of man he really is. This is deception.

The Trap of Offense:
What are offenses? **Offenses are crimes, wrongdoings, felonies, assaults, sins, and insults. They are the abuse and evil doings that others inflict on us.**

Forgiveness was the greatest test that I have had to overcome. **I had been undeservingly wronged and my grim reality left me discombobulated, gravely**

wounded and offended but God was asking me to forgive and let go. I knew I could forgive but letting go was an incontestable reality.

Joseph's response to his brother's betrayal is a prime example for us today and it was for me. His story taught me about godly character and how the Lord wanted me to respond to those who had hurt me **(Gen. 37-45).**

There is no doubt that in the earlier stages of my life, I would have wanted vengeance and would have carried it out. I lived by the motto, "an eye for an eye and a tooth for a tooth" and if I was Joseph, I would have probably been mapping out my revenge to settle the scores while sitting in my prison cell.

I am certain that Joseph had to fight the mental thoughts that raged against his brothers. Do not think for one minute that the devil did not bombard him with negative suggestions. I am convinced that Joseph was in constant battle to bring his emotions in check with the Word of God.

But in his obscurity, what do you think he needed to do? Trust. He had to frequently remind himself that God had the plan for his life. He remembered his dreams and the fact that if God had allowed him to suffer such unjustness, then there had to be a bigger plan; one that was unknown to him at the time.

The biggest fear factor in Christianity is a lack of trust. My advice is that in the obscurity of life, we should all do what Joseph did, <u>**stay focus**</u>. **Fight the good fight of faith! Hebrews 10:23** admonishes us to hold **fast the profession of our faith without wavering; for He is faithful that promised. But in verse 35, we are warned**

to not cast away our confidence. Why, because it has great reward. God is watching our response; for it is our attitude that determines the altitude.

Twenty years later, I finally understand the true meaning of the Great Commission of **Luke 4:18-19.** In this directive, I am charged with the assignment of ministering to the human soul whether the person is saved or not.

Jesus said through Apostle John that I overcome by the Blood of the Lamb and by the word of my testimony **(Rev. 12:11).** If you have no test, no trial, or tribulation, then you have no genuine proof, evidence, or testimony of God's bona fide and authentic power in your life. Unless I allowed Jesus to be my escape in my crisis, everything I went through would have been superficial thereby nullifying my testimony. My perception of God's Word would have only stemmed from a theological or a philosophical perspective.

When you can face and embrace Gethsemane and when you can boldly declare that you have done it God's way, uninterrupted by your so called great plans and ideas, then and only then will you see the resurrection power of God established in your life. Your life will yield the eternal fruit of the Holy Spirit that empowers you for living.

Retrospectively, when your crisis should have destroyed you and when you should have lost your mind, you will find that you can still stand clothed and graced in God's strength.

In times of adversity and especially when we are tempted to do things our way, we must remember to let

Jesus be our escape. The Lord will not allow us to be tempted above that which we can bear but with every temptation make a way of escape **(1 Cor. 10:13).**

He does not offer just any escape because He Himself is the escape. But His escape will not always fit our ideology and will sometimes cost us everything. It is the straight and narrow road and once you've entered through this humble gate, there is a mandate for righteousness, obedience, acceptance of persecution, love for enemies and self-denial.

Jesus, although whipped and beaten, did not stay in a defeated and hopeless state. He was crucified, died but then raised in victory and so will we. It is after we have been stricken and left for dead in our situation that God raises us in His power and strength unto victory.

Chapter 21

Mirror, Mirror, On the Wall …
Facing Myself

It took approximately two weeks before I could enter the room with mirrors. But I knew that if I were to carry on with my life, I would eventually need to confront what awaited me on the other side of the door. I made many attempts but I was overcome by fear each time. I needed the strength of the Most High to re-enter this room.

Finally, with much trepidation and a fear stricken heart, I made my way toward the door, reached for the doorknob, and at a snail's pace turned it. To my surprise beautiful lights immediately penetrated through. You could see the imperial rays that peered all the way through the corridor. I was awestruck by its beauty and each glare spellbound me.

As I stepped into the room, I could hear the echoes of their songs. I felt like a little girl that had been mesmerized by magic in a Disney movie. The mirrors possessed a riveting ambiance. Why was I so drawn to these mirrors? What hold did it have on me?

When I reached a few feet away from the mirrors, I observed that they were creatively and uniquely well thought-out. Each had the most intricate details and I wondered who the creator of these original and priceless masterpieces could be. I was filled with much wonder as I looked intently at the spectacular production.

All the mirrors were individually stunning and collectively they reflected a beauty that exuded a spectrum of perfection. It was a remarkable sight. But I noticed that each mirror depended on another mirror's element in order to project its glory. But the mirrors made me happy; they brought a sense of joy into my life. Oh, how I loved looking at the mirrors.

Compelled to take a closer look, I found that now its beauty no longer intrigued me. I hesitated because now instead of fascination, I felt uncomfortable and edgy. The mirrors now worried me and I did not know why. What would I see? What was I afraid of? I paused in fear but its entrancing magnetism wheedled me forward. With angst-ridden steps and a throbbing heart, I paced closer and closer. What would I find when I got close enough to see?

I reached toward the magnificent and dazzling display and anxiously removed one from its place. As I carefully held it in my hands, its numerous blemishes and defects were instantly revealed. I then examined other pieces only to find that many contained severe damages. They had been masked in the opulent simulations of beauty that they collectively projected and had gone undetected.

Propelled to take a long and deep stare into the mirror that I now held in my hands, I saw horrifying visions of the things I had tried so desperately to forget. The deformity of my composure was equivocal to that of the hunchback of Notre Dame and I appeared mutilated and defaced. I had been disfigured and scarred; it did not even look like me. But the Holy Spirit whispered, *"This is what you look like on the inside."* I shook in fear because the mirrors had depicted an accurate condition of my spiritual health.

Surely, that could not be me. I represented strength, beauty and confidence. But when I looked into the mirror, all I saw was a broken, feeble and wounded girl whose identity had been swathed in bandages. No longer able to withstand the heartache I felt, I hung the mirror back on the wall and walked out of the room in tears. I told myself that I would never return to this room.   I shut the door and left with my heart full of sorrow.

Chapter 22

The Potter's House

I was not on vacation or on break from ministry as some had supposed. No one knew what I was undergoing or that I had been a frequent visitor at the **Potter's House**. My journey had been a series of countless visits to this place, but this next visit would be quite unlike any other. I thought that I would have my small talks with the Father just as we had had in times past only to find that my quandary was a just cause to be immediately admitted into HECU (*Heaven's Emergency Care Unit*).

Rebukes from the Lord were oftentimes a result of my disobedience or carelessness in times past, but it was through these experiences that I learned many of life's valuable lessons. There were times I needed the Father's love or a whisper of comfort after a rebuke coupled with maybe a bandage or two. But this visit was very different, a bandage or two, a kiss on the check and a lollipop would not make these wounds go away. I knew that only my willingness to trust and keep going would bring me to my place of victory.

Facing the enemy in my time of adversity was mandatory if I wanted to competently achieve my goal. **The battle was a combat of life and death. Hell had forged this battle in desperation to nullify the call God in my life.** It was the rise to the next level, but I had to pass the test.

The test examined my fidelity and faith in God. I had to endure hardness as a good soldier of Jesus Christ **(2 Tim. 2:3)**. I had to undergo brutality, cruelty, harshness and difficulty just like a soldier would experience in a time of war, and above all, I was expected to outlast my enemy. I remembered Job.

The most critical point in the believer's life is when the enemy attacks what you care about the most. He seeks to come after something meaningful; something you deeply care about. But how many of us will faithfully outlast the turbulent storms that life brings? It is here, in this place of solitude that your dreams and aspirations are either birthed or aborted.

Think it not strange that you will suffer violence and major blows from your opponent. The enemy will attempt to assault every area of your life. You are no exception and you are not excused from his fiery darts. Your marriage, family, business, finances, health, mind and emotions will all be under attack. The Kingdom of Heaven suffers violence, but the violent take it by force **(Matt. 11:12).**

I was now forced to grow up and put everything I had learned into play. This was not an *I Declare War* card game and neither was it some childish board game. True war had been declared over my life, the life of my family and my seed. One very significant member of my family had been struck and I had to take my stand.

Chapter 23

The Potter's Wheel

I do not think anyone is ever ready for open-heart surgery. But I was neither prepared nor geared up for the ride on the *Potter's Wheel*. I had only heard about this place but I never imagined that my day of visitation would come.

My life, my dreams and my future were all contingent on my willingness to follow through. Just like the other places in my life, I dreaded this place also because it was also the place of decision. But my time had come and my case was before the Lord of Hosts. What would I choose to do now? Would I allow the Master to continue to break this already smitten vessel? Was I willing to pick up my cross and continue to follow Jesus?

There were many surgeries I underwent on the *Potter's Wheel*. I was not given sedatives to dull the pain that I would undergo; neither was I rewarded for being a brave girl. When I was allowed for home visits, I was not handed gifts, trophies or souvenirs to parade around. I was not given treasures from off the shelves of the *Potter's House* to indicate that I had been a guest of the Most Honored. In fact, all that could be seen were bandages, bruises and if you looked very, very closely you would even see some scars.

Many times when I thought I was put back into working order and ready to go, I found myself being re-admitted; each time into a different emergency room. This was the breaking point and the beginning of a new era in my life. My rubber had finally met the road.

By now I was in desperate pursuit to find this little Puerto Rican girl that I had hated so much; for she held the vital pieces to my life. But where was she and how could I find her? My God, what had I done to her?

Overcoming the Raging Storms:

As I came into view, I stood before a ferocious storm, and if the truth be told, I was scared to death as I gazed at the vast mammoth. There was a bridge to cross but the violent billows that suspended over the bridge indicated that there was great danger ahead.

Monstrous clouds opened their mouth and from it exhaled torrential vapors which sent chills up my spine. My helmet shifted and I could feel my feet buckling under me. Anxiety gripped my heart as the thoughts of being alone and without him flooded my mind once again. The dream we shared was no longer there, and I did not know how I would complete the rest of the journey without him.

As I inhaled the expanding smoky film, I sensed its toxic rush penetrating deep into my soul. Feeling cold, stiff and unable to move, I found myself being swallowed by the ground beneath me. My landing became slippery and wet as I soaked in the reality of my shattered world, and before I knew it, I was swooped away into the gulf of my tears and sorrow. **Waves of suicide thrashed vehemently at my head as I sought to die once again just like that dreadful day when I was fourteen years old.**

But the familiar cries that echoed from the distant shorelines broke through my dismal thoughts. I trailed the recognizable sounds to the water's edge near the bridge and there I glimpsed four little girls who had been washed up on the beachside. I do not know how they were able to withstand against the gushing tide or how long they had been there but their clothes looked tattered and old and you could tell they were wet, cold and very scared.

As I looked on, I was able to identify three of my children but the fourth child I could not discern. How did they get stranded on the beach? Were they swallowed up in the mouth of the sea just as I had been? I could sense the urgency as they desperately flagged their hands at me as if I had been an SOS ship who had come to the rescue. I paddled on in their direction as fast as I could and with each stroke uttered, *"I shall not die but live to declare the works of the Lord; I shall not die but live to declare the works of the Lord."*

In retaliation, the angered sea hurled her gigantic waves that plunged me underwater for long periods. They raged in fury when they saw my determination to reach the coast, and when I was not fighting the turbulent waves, I was contending with the underwater currents that were viciously trying to drag me further out into the sea.

My Determination to Live and not Die:

One moment of self-pity and selfishness had led me away from the shorelines of safety and reason and into a dejected and hopeless glut. **But the thoughts of leaving my children to face the enemy without me caused me to triumph above the tide each time. I**

refused to quit and leave them destitute, alone and afraid. My work was not finished and I was not about to disappoint them by giving up on life. **God had given them to me and it was up to me to forever break the cycle of rejection and abandonment that was now trying so hard to infiltrate their lives.** I had to defeat this monster, if not, the undefeated ogre would haunt them the rest of their lives just as it had done to me.

My love for them somehow elevated me over the waves and thrust me onto the shorelines. I was exhausted and worn out but at last I had reached my children. By now, the torrential storm had subsided and everything appeared calm and beautiful. Their appearance had changed and they were undisturbed and at ease as if nothing had ever happened. Their clothes were not torn and old as I had observed earlier and the sun was now shining down on them. When I turned to look for the fourth girl, I did not see her. I asked them what happened to her but they answered that no one else had been with them.

Back to the Room with Mirror, Mirror on the Wall:

My beautiful room of mirrors was only a shadow of what had been. The beautiful ambiance and riveting glories were my past. It was the spectrum of perfection of the world I had created, yet, a false perception for my present condition. I now knew that as long as I allowed the mirrors to remain on the wall, I would stay in the time zone of my past and never move forward into the greater things God had waiting for me.

I no longer wanted to look at the mirrors because the beauty I once knew was fading with each passing moment. I did not want to be here and now I hated the mirrors that I had once thought to be so beautiful.

I stared in horror as a sick and overwhelming feeling overtook me. I dropped the mirror that I held in my hands shattering it into a thousand pieces. I ran toward the wall and grabbed at another mirror, but it too depicted the same repulsive image. I was pain-stricken because they conveyed the unchanged chronicled of my devastated state over and over.

The pain was too great and the temptation of getting hold of a mirror that chronicle my riveting past was very enticing. I went on a rapid searched for the one that would bring me to the glory I once knew. Just one more look, one more moment would give me the quick fix I needed to dull the pain I wanted so desperately to cease. But the chance of being trapped and lost forever in the mirror would mean abandoning the call of God on my life and the life of my children.

I continued my pursuit of grabbing at the mirrors and striking them onto the floor until there were no mirrors left on the wall. I lay hysterically sobbing because the mirrors had spoken the truth; a truth I was not willing to face until this moment. There were no more mirrors and no more hiding places. The REAL ME no longer had a choice now but to stand up!

Chapter 24

A Willingness to Rise Up and Walk

It is when I began to walk closely with men and women in church leadership that I began to see how many of God's people are in a state of crisis. But because of shame and fear of rejection, they hide behind their pretentious masks just as I had done. They wallow through their personal issues alone and afraid; never getting the full release of healing and deliverance they so deserve.

Unfortunately, many churches in America today have sadly become a superficial, social gathering, traditionally dogmatic system that is comprised of nothing more than religious nuts who think that by keeping perfect church attendance, wearing doilies on their heads, and quoting scripture will get them into Heaven; many have become so heavenly-minded that they are no earthly good.

No wonder the world looks at us with mockery. We have become lost and imprisoned in our own unrealistic Christian fantasy while the world around us sadly suffers much in the same way. Like drug addicts, we live in denial; never fully blossoming in the abundance of God. We have become prisoners of our own doctrines and beliefs and hindered by our traditions and way of thinking.

If we take an honest look inside, we will find that most of us do not function to our full potential. Many of us never give birth to the spiritual babies we carry and many of our dreams are often aborted. Why, because we have not genuinely dealt with the issues that keep us from becoming who God said we already are.

Suppressing, ignoring or pretending that our problems do not exist only delays God's healing. I had to keep my eyes fixed on the prize and remind myself of the promises of the Father. I am so thankful that God is forever merciful and longsuffering. For today, I would not have the opportunity to walk in my destiny.

In Joshua's days, God's people faced physical giants. **Today, the giants we fight are spiritual and they dwell in the land of our mind and soul.** This is why we are warned in **2 Corinthians 10:5** about taking responsibility for our **thought-life. II Chronicles 7:14** says that when we humble ourselves, pray and seek His face, and turn from our wicked ways that He will hear from heaven and will forgive our sins and heal our land. God will not allow us to come to the next level of our calling until we confront the giants in our lives and permit His power to bring them down. We cannot conquer what we fail to confront.

Most of the children of Israel died in the wilderness and went home before their time because their mindsets would not change. God did not allow them to see the fulfillment of the promise land because every time Israel lost sight of her identity as the covenant people, the nation plunged into repeated cycles of spiritual, moral and social disorder with *"every man doing that which was right in his own eyes"* **(Judges 21:25)**. He would only allow the new generation of His people to come into the promise land.

No one ever comes to his or her full potential in comfort zone. If we reject the breaking process we face the danger of contaminating the baby (ministry) God gives us by imparting to them what is on us. What is on the head will flow onto the body. It is God's desire to heal our land (soul), but we cannot triumph over what we refuse to meet head on.

There was a man that sat at the beautiful pool of Bethesda in **John chapter 5**. He sat around with others just like him for thirty-eight years because it was expected that an angel would come down at a certain season to trouble the waters. Whosoever therefore stepped into the water first was healed of whatever disease he had. When the Lord Jesus came around and healed the man, the religious leaders began to persecute both Jesus and the man. These leaders were bound by their religious traditions of men and because Jesus had performed the healing on the Sabbath, they were all bent out of shape about it.

How many of us are like that man; waiting for someone else to help us out of our bad situation instead of pulling from the strength within through the power of Jesus Christ. **When asked by Jesus if he wanted to be made whole, he completely disregarded the question and made excuses as to why he had not been healed. He almost missed his opportunity because he was accustomed to the traditional way of thinking; always waiting for someone to help him.** Too often we linger in our dead-end situation in hopes that someone will come to our aid. But until we face the reality of our situation and take up our own bed and walk, we will sit yet another thirty-eight years.

Chapter 25

Gethsemane's Butterfly

The **Garden of Gethsemane** brings about a major crisis; one that will shake us in the very roots of our life. This was what Gethsemane was for the Lord Jesus and it will be just that for every believer. My life had been deracinated into an emotional crucifixion. I was betrayed, rejected, misunderstood, morally lonely and now all alone with my God.

Gethsemane means *oil-press* and in Gethsemane, you will suffer under intense pressure. This is the place where your flesh, your will, and your desires are literally crushed. Your flesh encounters brutal assaults of every kind in preparation of its crucifixion and death. You encounter powerful resistance from your insides that refuses to face death and its indescribable loneliness. It plunges in full force to wrestle against your spirit, and its only desire and goal is to outlive the slaughter so that God's purpose and plan for your life never come to fruition.

The purpose for Gethsemane is to realize and accept that there is no other way but God's way. Gethsemane's aim is to uproot the old and plant a new way of life. How can new life occur without dying? But must I die in this manner? Why death and humiliation? Could there be some other way? If Jesus felt anything like I did, I am sure He asked the same questions when He was faced with Gethsemane.

In my studies of butterflies, I found that only a small number of them spin silken cocoons around themselves in preparation for its next phase of life.

Before beginning the transformation process into a pupa, the caterpillar spits out weaves of silk to be used to make its cocoon or new home. The silk then hardens into a tough solid shell.

The exoskeleton or outer skin then begins to tear near its head, and the pupa begins to emerge. As the exoskeleton falls, the pupa plunges a many-hooked structure at the end of its belly and into the pad. This established method is dangerous and can be fatal for the pupa because if it does not grip at the pad fast enough, the pupa may fall to the ground and die.

The silken thread is the only harness that holds the pupa upside down in its final stage and just before his breakthrough. Just as a pupa will cling for its life, so held I to the Word of God. I emitted the Word of God out of my mouth and it created for me a cocoon or shelter to shield me during my transformation process.

The *logos* or the *written Word of God* was my essential food and it is what kept me alive. The bread of life that I digested in my earlier stages of growth (like the caterpillar) would be what I would now in turn regurgitate and discharge. I allowed the old way of thinking (the exoskeleton) to be broken; remember, the split begins near the head so it had to begin with my thought life. I began to live by the words that proceeded out of God's mouth by transferring them into my mouth because the **power of life and death was in my tongue (Proverbs 18:21).**

Because the pupa is motionless during this time, it is said to be in a "resting stage." But don't be fooled, for much activity is occurring inside of the cocoon;

something extraordinary is taking place inside the caterpillar. The larval formation of the undeveloped pupa are being broken down and reforming into those of an adult butterfly. Though this phase appears to be the worst time in the caterpillar's life, it is actually the most wonderful. It is revamping into something extraordinary; something that it has never been.

Can you see your life much like the butterfly? How many times have our beliefs, rules and way of thinking been broken down by our Gethsemane experience only to be converted or renewed by a new order of God's Word?

When we see chaos and confusion all around, we can respond in two ways. We can grumble and disempower ourselves with a sense of depression and hopelessness or we can choose to see this as an external forewarning that the old order is collapsing, breaking up and waiting to be transformed into a level of new-sprung vicissitude.

Has your life ever been turned upside down, but because you allowed the Word of God to dominate your thinking, people say you are glowing? Another word for cocoon is chrysalis. The word *chrysalis* comes from the Greek word **chrysos**, which means gold. Even in its upside down transformation stage and what appears to be the worst time in the caterpillar's life, the chrysalis produces a shimmering gold appearance. Your pupa stage will transform you into His image once you stayed the course and allow the Word of God to govern your life.

After the adult butterfly has taken shape, its body then gives off fluids that loosen it from the pupal casing and the thorax expands causing the shell to split wide open. **Our lives should be so full of the Spirit and Word of God that it literally breaks through any obstacle that hinders us from fulfilling our dreams.**

The head and thorax are the first to emerge. Next, the butterfly pushes its legs out and pulls the rest of its body free. **Notice that the head emerges first. This is important to note because a renewed mind will break through any obstacle and thrust you out of any situation.** You can withstand any stress the devil sends your way.

After this stage, our life should give off a delightful aroma and our lives should be like fruit yielding trees where people can pick, eat and live from. The fruit of the Spirit is produced from our personal experiences.

Gethsemane awaits us all. But when it does happen and it will happen, it is helpful to remember that we are inside a new womb, undergoing a new gestation and waiting for new birth.

My Personal Gethsemane:

But Gethsemane is a lonely place; a place where those closest to you will fall asleep on you, just as the disciples fell asleep on Jesus. Your so called best friends fall into slumber in your darkest hour of need. While many go on with their lives, you are out of sight, out of mind and alone to face your Gethsemane. Some will stay behind and watch from a distance, some praying and cheering for you while others watch to see what will become of you.

Like Jesus, I too was faced with my Gethsemane experience. I had some indication of what I was about to contend with and it seemed insurmountable, unjust and unfair. Why had God permitted this to happen? Could there not be another way?

As I lay before the Lord mourning and grieving for the loss I had just suffered, I told the Lord that I could not face this alone. It was a bitter cup to drink from. My flesh did not want to drink of it because His way seemed too hard. But all God would say was, *"Daughter, the only way out is to go through; the only way out is to go through."*

In Gethsemane, my will was unmistakably brought to a state of consistent brokenness every time; my flesh, however, with all its narcissistic rights tried desperately to hang on with everything it had. It got ugly; for here, I often came to blows with the anger, bitterness, resentment and unforgiveness I thought I had overcome. These quadruplet siblings walked hand in hand and would often surface when things were not going my way, when I was losing control or when I thought God was moving too slow; again, a neglect of **2 Corinthians 10:5.**

I was taken aback when the Holy Spirit began to show me what He found hidden behind the curtains of my inner self. The real fight was on as each strongman was exposed. **Pomposity often revealed its obnoxious and hideous ways, and in desperation tried to hide its ugly face; but it was no match in the light of Jesus.**

God was now asking me to lay down my rights to be hurt and offended for the last time. **Who inflicted my hurt was no longer the issue. My real test was in** releasing and forgiving those that had wounded me. **If I was to mirror my Father, I had to release and forgive my offenders without any hang-ups or strings attached.** I was learning about the unadulterated agape love of God.

But make no mistake, my flesh and spirit went to war every time a strongman was recognized, and each time they caused a spiritual upheaval. **The spirit of heaviness that often times swathed itself around me had pledged to never leave me alone.** I experienced abnormal states of perpetual grief and for months I underwent excessive mourning and sorrow. **I suffered from insomnia and depression, and my inner hurts blistered excessively, often times leaving me in oozes of despair and loneliness. My prolonged state of hopelessness robbed my joy of living, which led to self-pity, depression, and then thoughts of suicide.**

Many times I felt scared and all alone once again, just like that little girl I had buried years ago. But this was my cross and my storm and I had to decide if I was going to be pitiful or powerful; but I knew I could not be both. I had to decide if I was going to take God at His Word, ride out the storm and fight or relinquish my constitutional Biblical rights, surrender and permit the enemy to confiscate everything that belonged to me. Would I hide my face from the world and its vicious criticisms or would I allow the resurrection power of God to turn my dead end situation around?

But the ultimate conflict was battled in my mind. My problems promoted my spiritual maturity; for they sharpened my ability to engage in spiritual combat. My victory was contingent upon my steadfast, unshakeable, consistent and relentless faith-based prayers.

I learned to prevail over the battering assaults of my thought life and to refute the disparaging feedback that concurred with my fickle emotions. Although victory was undeniably guaranteed, I had to remember that my emotions were fickle, unreliable, and very deceiving. But with determination, stamina, a refusal to accept defeat, and an indomitable posture to push beyond this point, I won many battles.

The Gates of Gethsemane:

I have passed through the gates of Gethsemane; the kneeling place. Sometimes I still pray, *"Please let this cup pass,"* but it always ends with, *"Not my will but yours be done."* Please understand that passing through the gate does not mean you will never return. For it seems as if one never truly stops visiting the Garden of Gethsemane for good; there are continual revisit to this place of dying to self.

Victory or defeat was contingent upon my determination to triumph over this obstacle. This was the focal point of the examination and I wanted an A+. All hell gaped in bewilderment as I opted to dig my heels into the ground, confront, oppose and stand firm against their unending ferociously sadistic threats. They had created a godly-monster out of me and I was mad as hell. They failed to remember that Narda Martinez was no quitter, and I was not about to go out like that!

Heaven cheered on!

Chapter 26

The Vision

I was in Atlantic City when the Lord spoke to me out of the book of **Habakkuk 2**. I knew the vision, I had seen it and now God was telling me to write it down.

What is vision? **Vision is a mental image, picture or revelation of your future state. Vision is a bridge that will take you from your present and into your future.** When God spoke to me, He spoke to me out of my destiny and future, not my past or existing and present condition. But how would I now bring the vision that He had given me into reality? I need a strategy; I needed a plan.

First, He told me to write my vision down. One Sunday morning, the Holy Spirit awakened me about 5:30 a.m. I remember jumping off my cot; it was as if time had again stood still as He gave me the instructions I needed to make the dream He had given a reality. The Holy Spirit told me that I would not only write a book but perform a musically dramatized account of it.

The vision was made distinctively clear; there was no doubt to what I had seen and heard and I was excited. I immediately went to work on my computer. As I made a start to put the pieces of the vision on paper, I began to get a revelation of who I really was, what I was created for, and the real reason for my existence—the why? I know knew that I was created for the purpose in plan in the mind of God. The God that had the blueprints for my life had defined me long before I was ever a thought in my parent's mind or a seed in my mother's womb. I was supplied with whatever skills and creativity I needed to get the job done. With a constant reminder of this revelation in my thought life, through Him I could do everything I needed to do.

I often told my students that their talent is a gift from God, but what they do with their talent was their gift to God. What would I now do with the gifts that had been placed in my hands? How would I implement them? My operation needed an objective; my mission needed a goal.

A goal is a vision with a plan. The vision had to be made evident, clear, and copyrighted. The Scripture states that without a vision the people perish **(Proverbs 29:18).** I had to clearly define my goals and objectives because if I didn't, my vision would not come to pass. **Without a goal, my vision would be nothing more than a dream;** so I set daily goals, mapped my success and allowed the Holy Spirit to give it direction.

One thing that I love about Jesus is that He never allowed what happened to Him or what others said to dictate who He was. Even in His moment of betrayal, He was confident about his assignment.

Jesus' mission clearly made it known who He was; the Son of God who came to seek, save and restore lives. Why? **John 3:16** tells us that, **"For God so loved the world that He gave His only Son."** The Lord Jesus knew that the Father had sent Him for the purpose of bringing salvation to a lost and dying world.

Write the Vision and Make it Plain:
Likewise, my mission became my purpose and drive; it

defined who I was, what I was created for and why. But it was equally as important that the vision be clear so that others could read it and run with it **(Hab. 2:2)**.

The word *others* in this verse is key. Many years ago, I worked as a traveling sales representative for a company that sold an all-purpose cleaner. For those who know anything about the sales/marketing business, you know that people buy into the leader. The leader of a business or organization must have a mission statement in place in order to effectively broadcast or make public its reason for its existence, its function and its target.

Your mission statement is your *who*, your *what*, and your *why*. Just as a manufacturer would have a purpose and goal for its invention, God created me with a purpose. Everything about me had become a message but if I could not communicate my vision, it would be ineffective.

My vision needed support, aid and encouragement. **I Corinthians 15:33** reveals that we become the product of what we are around. Teamwork is what makes the dream work. As I began to pray, God began to send people who were likeminded my way. I networked with people who celebrated the gifts and call of God upon my life. My mentors were very encouraging and would often let me know that I could do it, I could have it and that through Christ I could do all things.

Birthing the Vision:
I approached each step as an assignment, and two days later, I finished the project. I placed them in

trendy folders that I bought from Staples and I made an appointment to meet with my pastors.

Passion and determination became the driving force that propelled my vision into fruition. I became passionate about the call of God on my life and as a result, my dreams became motivated, stimulated and finally alive.

But the battle deepened as I began to execute and put into operation my plan of action. And now that I had the strategy, the enemy plunged in full force against me. What would I do with the vision God had given me? All hell had broken loose against me and now I was left with nothing but a vision and a dream that was a hundred times greater than me.

I had entered the waiting process, and at this stage of development, you are like that pupa that is literally hanging upside down, clinging to its very life; grasping at the only thing that can hold it together and keep it from falling to the ground. You feel the intense pressure as the world you knew begins to fall apart. You are confined to this lonely place, a place that has been reserved for you and you only. You and all that you have ever known begin to mutate. You begin to shed your exoskeleton as the old order begins to be broken down into tiny fragments until there is nothing left. Only your main organs remain and the new shell that now encases you begins to harden.

But as the pressure intensified, I held firm and did not quit. I stayed the course as I kept on trusting and believing; I held hope against hope as I kept running to reach the prize. I was determined to finish what God started whether I was celebrated or not. **I held on even when I was rejected, abandoned and betrayed because for the first time in my life, I genuinely understood who I was.** I had resolved that nothing was going to prevent me from fulfilling my purpose. My tenacity to make it thrust me forward like bullet shot from a pistol.

I was always known to have crazy, radical faith. But faith is not something you focus on or some energy you try to grab; it is not material or stuff you can hold but rather, something God gives that empowers you to believe and receive what He said. Faith simply believes. The Scripture clearly states that through faith we overcome the world **(1 John 4:4).**

Although the waiting process is the most difficult when God gives you a vision and you remain steadfast, if you do not quit but dig your heals firmly into the ground, if you stay the course and keep believing though the odds are stack greatly against you, God will begin to pour out the blessing.

Remember that faithfulness and obedience will always open the door for God's favor. Your perseverance and determination to disallow the enemy to snuff you out will always pay high dividends. Once you have been planted, it is at this point that your leaf does not wither and whatsoever you do prospers (Psalm 1). God then begins to multiply you, expand you and in your season, you bring forth the reward of the Lord.

Vision has a voice that speaks. It told me to keep hope alive and believe through the toughest times of my life. It told me to speak and frame my world

with the Word of my mouth. Vision said to speak to the "nothings" and the chaos and disorders in my life. I called those things that were not as though they were and as I did, I began to witness the same creative powerful result as my heavenly Father. **Job 22** says *"to declare it, say it, and it shall be established."* I shouted it, I cried it, I sang it and **I continued to confess what I believed until it finally materialized.**

The Power of Faith:

As my faith soared, it became a divine influence that pulled me away from unbelief and doubt and straight into victory. It adjusted my mindset to accept victory and to stop settling for the defeat I often encountered. Eventually, it produced in me an indefatigable posture to stand with the Word of God that had been spoken prophetically over my life; creating in me an ability to rely solely on His power and not my own. This was my season and I was unwaveringly determined to be pulled out of the quicksand of fear. I made a sound decision to accept that I was born of God and that I had the very means of success already in me.

Chapter 27

The Abraham Walk

A major turn of events had now taken place. After facing many intense and spiritual battles in New York and coping with a failing marriage, I thought I was being presumptuous when I booked a one-way ticket to Georgia. I would later discover that God had allowed a spiritual whirlwind to take place causing me to make what many thought to be an 'imprudent jump.'

I was scared as I somehow felt in my heart that I would not return to New York. How would I survive when I got to Georgia? I had little money and three girls to look after. But this was my "Abraham walk." God was calling me out of the familiar and into the unknown. He was asking me to give up everything; the house, the marriage, the school, my friends, my goals, my dreams and ultimately my life as I had known it to be.

I was instructed to gather my most important documents and I was only allowed to take one luggage and my laptop; it was the same for the children. I asked the Lord how I was to get all my shoes into the one bag; surely my shoes alone would require a luggage or two but I heard again, only one luggage.

My heart was thumping as we quickly packed in the dark; for up to now we still had no lights. He was due to pass by soon and I wanted to be gone to avoid any altercation.

I was too scared to cry as we made our way to the airport. We got there only to find that our flight had been canceled for the next day. I knew we could not go home so I asked the girls to get ready for a long and uncomfortable night. We pulled the chained seats together and it became our bed.

When we finally got on the plane the next day, I wondered how life would turn out. I was now a single mother with three children. What would become of us?

Join us as we continue our faith adventures in the sequel, **When My Life Struck Twelve.** In this sequel, you will encounter our adventures in the House of Prophets, crazy mission trips, humility classes, miracles, a Brook of Cherith experience and a path that leads me to my kinsman redeemer, my Boaz.

Conclusion

The trials in my life have helped me to find the character, personality and the grace of God. Along the way, I have found some of the precious gems the psalmist wrote about. These rare and extraordinary stones are not the kind you see at prominent showrooms or buy at prestigious shops. They are original and priceless and have been purchased through my painful experiences.

I came to know the Father's love through the most difficult and trying times of my life. My trials only came to make me strong and strong I will be as long as I hold to the One who holds my hand.

I am forever a student and a servant of the Most High God. As Paul said, *"I speak not as though I had already attained, either were already perfect: but I follow after, if that I may apprehend that for which also I am apprehended for Christ Jesus. For my brothers and sisters, I count not myself to have apprehended: but this one thing I do, forgetting those things which are behind, and reaching forth unto those things which are before. I press toward the mark for the prize of the high calling of God in Christ Jesus"* (Philippians 3:12-14).

There are higher heights and deeper depths. There will always be new levels to achieve, higher mountains to cross over and deeper valleys to walk through. Take every opportunity as a step toward your destiny. Overcome your challenges and learn from your mistakes; love deeply and forgive genuinely. An anonymous writer once said, *"A successful person is one who can lay a firm foundation with the bricks others throw at him."*

An Update on Narda—a Husband's Perspective:

I believe that what the devil meant for evil against Narda, God turned for good because when I married her, I received God's special blessing—**a true Proverbs 31 woman!** God used her personal struggles to prepare her for me and for His people because now, she is not only my beloved wife and the first lady of Whitewright, Texas, but she is God's special vessel who is powerfully anointed to minister to His people.

Narda and her new husband; Mayor Bill Goodson

To His Glory Publishing

Let Us Publish Your Book

To His Glory Publishing Company will publish your book at the least expensive cost. We pay one of the highest royalties in the industry – 40%! We print on demand and place your book on the major online bookstores such a Amazon.com, Barnesandnoble.com, Bookamillion.com, etc.

WWW.TOHISGLORYPUBLISHING.COM
(770) 458-7947

TO HIS GLORY PUBLISHING COMPANY, INC.

463 Dogwood Dr. Lilburn, GA. 30047, U.S.A (770)458-7947

Order Form for Bookstores in the USA

Order Date: _____

Order Placed By: _____   By Fax: _____

Address: _____

_____

City _____ ST/ZIP _____

Phone #: _____

Email: _____

Purchase Order#: _____

Return Policy: Within 1 year but not before 90 Days.

Price	Quantity	List Price
Shipping Method:		
Media:		
UPS:		
FedEx:		
Other (Please Secify):		
Total Price:	**Total Quantity:**	**List Price**

Ship To Address: Bill to Address:

CPSIA information can be obtained at www.ICGtesting.com
Printed in the USA
BVOW011143100612

292233BV00007B/57/A